The **Eating Disorders** Update

Titles in the DISEASE UPDATE series:

DISEASE
UPDATE

The **Eating Disorders** Update
Understanding Anorexia, Bulimia, and Binge Eating

Alvin and Virginia Silverstein and Laura Silverstein Nunn

Enslow Publishers, Inc.
40 Industrial Road
Box 398
Berkeley Heights, NJ 07922
USA

http://www.enslow.com

Acknowledgments

The authors thank Chris L. Ohlemeyer, M.D., Associate Professor, Pediatrics, and Director, Adolescent Medicine, Saint Louis University School of Medicine, and Karyn L. Scher, Ph.D., a licensed psychologist in Pennsylvania, for their careful reading of the manuscript and their many helpful comments and suggestions.

Library of Congress Cataloging-in-Publication Data

Silverstein, Alvin.
  The eating disorders update : understanding anorexia, bulimia, and binge eating / Alvin and Virginia Silverstein and Laura Silverstein Nunn.
    p. cm.— (Disease update)
  Summary: "An introduction to the history and most up-to-date research and treatment of eating disorders"—Provided by publisher.
  Includes bibliographical references and index.
  ISBN-13: 978-0-7660-2802-9
  ISBN-10: 0-7660-2802-X
  1. Eating disorders—Juvenile literature. 2. Compulsive eating—Juvenile literature. 3. Anorexia nervosa—Juvenile literature. 4. Bulimia—Juvenile literature. I. Silverstein, Virginia B. II. Nunn, Laura Silverstein. III. Title.

RC552.E18S546 2008

616.85'26—dc22

2007013985

Printed in the United States of America

10 9 8 7 6 5 4 3 2 1

To Our Readers: We have done our best to make sure all Internet Addresses in this book were active and appropriate when we went to press. However, the author and the publisher have no control over and assume no liability for the material available on those Internet sites or on other Web sites they may link to. Any comments or suggestions can be sent by e-mail to comments@enslow.com or to the address on the back cover.

♻ Enslow Publishers, Inc., is committed to printing our books on recycled paper. The paper in every book contains 10% to 30% post-consumer waste (PCW). The cover board on the outside of each book contains 100% PCW. Our goal is to do our part to help young people and the environment too!

Photo Credits: Associated Press, pp. 12, 18, 23, 31, 72, 86, 88, 93; © Bubbles Photolibrary/Alamy, p. 55; © Corel Corporation, p. 30; Courtesy Dr. Catherine Steiner-Adair, p. 97; © David Young-Wolff/Alamy, p. 40; Getty Images, pp. 22, 42; iStockphoto.com/Cat London, p. 38 (bottom); iStockphoto.com/Nathan Blaney, p. 27; © John Birdsall/The Image Works, p. 62; © 2007 Jupiterimages Corporation, pp. 14, 43, 44, 45; Mark A. Philbrick/BYU, p. 78; Mauro Fermariello/Photo Researchers, Inc., p. 82; © Michael Newman/Photo Edit, p. 8; © Paramount Television/Courtesy: Everett Collection, p. 24; Phanie/Photo Researchers, Inc., p. 34; Ron Tom/© ABC/Courtesy: Everett Collection, p. 91; Scott Camazine & Sue Trainor/Photo Researchers, Inc., p. 37; Shutterstock, pp. 5, 16, 38 (top), 39, 52, 53, 68, 101; © Sonda Dawes/The Image Works, p. 102; U.S. Department of Agriculture, p. 100.

Cover Photos: David Young-Wolff/Alamy

Publisher's Note: While the stories of people affected by eating disorders in this book are real, many of the names have been changed.

Contents

Eating Disorders

What are they?

Eating disorders are mental health conditions characterized by extreme and dangerous eating habits. There are three main types: anorexia nervosa, bulimia, and binge eating disorder (also called compulsive overeating). *Anorexia* typically involves severe weight loss due to self-starvation. *Bulimia* typically involves eating large amounts of food (bingeing) and then getting rid of it by vomiting, using laxatives or diuretics (purging), or by fasting or exercising excessively. *Binge eating disorder* involves uncontrollable urges to eat large amounts of food in a short amount of time. It often leads to obesity.

Who gets them?

People of all ages, all ethnic groups, and both males and females. More than 90 percent of the cases, however, are girls and women between the ages of twelve and thirty-five. Eating disorders are becoming increasingly common in children under twelve years old. In addition, they have been affecting an increasing number of boys and young men.

How do you get them?

The exact causes are not known. A number of factors may be involved, including genetic, biological, psychological, and social influences. Eating disorders often start with the desire to be thin and dieting that gradually becomes more extreme.

What are the signs or symptoms?

Anorexia: dramatic and severe weight loss, extreme tiredness, refusal to eat. *Bulimia:* trips to the bathroom right after every meal (purging is often secretive). *Binge eating disorder:* extreme overweight (obesity).

How are they treated?

A combination of psychotherapy, medication, family therapy, and nutrition counseling. Serious cases may need hospitalization and/or around-the-clock treatment in a residential eating disorders clinic.

How can they be prevented?

Education is the main tool for preventing eating disorders. It is also helpful to learn healthy eating habits and ways to improve self-esteem. A well-balanced diet and moderate exercise can help people stay at a healthy weight.

As many as 70 million people worldwide suffer from eating disorders every year. Most of them are girls and women between the ages of twelve and thirty-five.

1

A Battle With Food

IN THE FALL OF 2004, Alice and Peter Marks could not believe their eyes as they watched their daughter, Lisa, performing onstage in her school play. Under the bright spotlights, Alice saw her daughter in a new light. Lisa looked very thin and weak. She had sunken cheeks, and her face was pale. There were dark circles under her eyes. Alice knew that Lisa had lost weight recently, but she had no idea how much—until now. Alice had to face the possibility that her daughter—at only ten years old—had an eating disorder.

Alice and Peter did not know how to help their daughter get better. After the school play, Lisa was even more focused on her weight. Although her family told her she looked very thin, Lisa was convinced she was fat.

She then put herself on a starvation diet. Over the next five weeks, her parents took her to see the school psychologist, the family pediatrician, and a private therapist. They all agreed that she had an eating disorder called anorexia nervosa. It was a serious threat to her health, but no one could get her to believe it. Lisa continued to lose weight. Her parents begged her to eat. They even tried to bribe her, promising they would buy her a pony. At dinnertime, Lisa would eat just a few spoonfuls before saying she was finished. Food was a constant battle in the Marks household.

By Christmas, Lisa had become so weak that she hardly left the couch. A few days after New Year's, her worried parents took her to the emergency room. Lisa was immediately hooked up to an IV, which helped replace the lost body fluids. A week later, she was back home—and back to starving herself. It wasn't long before she wound up in the hospital again. Lisa's parents realized that in order for Lisa to get better, she would need round-the-clock treatment.

In February 2005, Lisa was taken to a residential eating disorders clinic in Omaha, Nebraska. This was one of the few facilities in the country that treated young children with eating disorders. Lisa stayed there for two months. Gradually, she managed to gain weight. Her mother stayed in a nearby hotel. She joined her daughter in weekly therapy sessions that were designed to include her in Lisa's treatment. When Lisa returned home, she was homeschooled until she could get her strength back.

By the fall, everything had changed for the Marks family. As Lisa started sixth grade, she was feeling better than she had in a long time. She still looked thin, but she was slowly gaining weight. She was good about eating her three meals a day, and having three or four snacks as well. However, Lisa admits that it is still an ongoing struggle. There are times when her old feelings—that food is the enemy—are still lurking in the back of her mind. But her mother is very proud of her. One day, Alice was surprised to see her daughter putting sour cream on a baked potato. It was then that Alice realized that Lisa was on the road to a healthier life.[1]

A Growing Health Threat

Eating disorders have become a serious problem all over the world. Mental health agencies do not know exactly how many people suffer from these disorders, since many cases go unreported because of shame or denial.

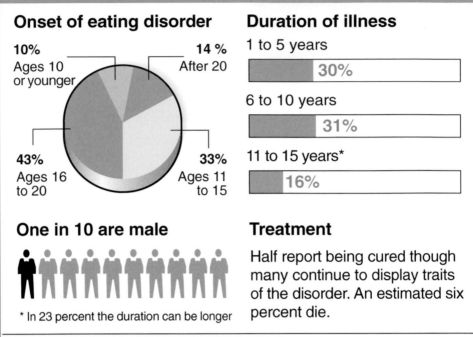

Onset of eating disorder

10%
Ages 10
or younger

14 %
After 20

43%
Ages 16
to 20

33%
Ages 11
to 15

One in 10 are male

* In 23 percent the duration can be longer

Duration of illness

1 to 5 years

| 30% |

6 to 10 years

| 31% |

11 to 15 years*

| 16% |

Treatment

Half report being cured though many continue to display traits of the disorder. An estimated six percent die.

SOURCE: National Association of Anorexia Nervosa and Associated Disorders   AP

However, researchers have made some estimates. Worldwide, in any given year, as many as 70 million people struggle with an eating disorder. In the United States, up to 24 million people are affected.[2] Most of them are girls and women, ages twelve to thirty-five.[3] The condition is much less common in boys and men, who account for about 10 to 15 percent of the cases.[4] Many people who have eating disorders do not realize or admit they have a problem.

Alice Marks still blames herself for not getting help for Lisa sooner. "It was right in front of me," she says, "but I just didn't realize that children could get an eating disorder this young."[5] Alice's thinking is understandable, considering the statistics showing that eating disorders are not typically seen in girls as young as ten. This trend could be changing, however. Since 2000, doctors and mental health specialists have reported an increasing number of cases involving children ages seven to thirteen. In addition, researchers have learned that eating disorders are becoming increasingly common among boys and young men.

Many teenagers, especially girls, believe that looking good will make them popular. The constant images of skinny models in magazines and good-looking people on TV and in the movies give a false idea of what people are supposed to look like. Some young people figure that if they look thin, then others will like them more. That is not necessarily true. In fact, this kind of thinking can be harmful. Some people worry about their weight

> Worldwide, in any given year, as many as 70 million people struggle with an eating disorder. In the United States, up to 24 million people are affected.

Food for Life

People cannot live without food. The foods we eat supply the fuel for energy to help us walk, read, think, and all the other things we do every day. The amount of energy in food is measured in calories. Food also provides building materials to grow and to repair damaged and worn-out body parts.

All food is made up of chemicals called nutrients. The basic kinds of nutrients are proteins, carbohydrates, fats, vitamins, minerals, and water. Different amounts of these nutrients can be found in a variety of food groups—grains, fruits, vegetables, meats, dairy products, and fats and sweets. Nutrition experts say that people need to eat a balanced diet to stay healthy. (A balanced diet is one that supplies enough of a variety of foods, within a healthy range of calories.) When people do not get the right nutrition, they may become tired and weak, have problems thinking clearly, and might even get sick.

constantly. They may be terrified of gaining weight. Frequent warnings about the dangers of being overweight and statistics on "obesity in America" only add to these worries. The pressures young people feel to be thin may lead to an unrealistic fear or hatred of food, resulting in some serious eating problems.

More and more teenagers are dieting to lose weight. Medical experts worry that when young people diet, they may not be getting all the calories and important nutrients that their bodies need to grow. Some kids develop dangerous eating habits. These habits may become so extreme that they lead to an eating disorder.

There are three main types of eating disorders:

Anorexia nervosa. Anorexia nervosa is a condition in which people become obsessed with being thin and refuse to eat enough food to keep them healthy.

Bulimia. Bulimia is a condition in which people binge (eat large amounts of food in a short period of time) and then purge (get rid of the extra calories by making themselves throw up, by taking laxatives, or by overexercising).

Binge eating disorder. Often called *compulsive overeating,* this is a condition in which people eat huge amounts of food, but unlike bulimics, they do not purge. This eating disorder can lead to obesity—being seriously overweight. For some kids, the stresses in their lives are so overwhelming that they may turn to food as comfort. An increasing number of kids are becoming obese. The medical community is worried because

Downsizing

Modern society puts a lot of importance on being thin. Many people worry about fitting into a size 0 like the skinny supermodels. Knowing that they need to wear a bigger size can be depressing. Some clothing designers have come up with a way to make people *feel* thin. They have lowered the size on clothing labels, in what has been known as "vanity sizing," to make the customer feel better. So somebody who used to wear size 12 jeans can now fit into a size 8. Many customers who shop at the stores that sell these downsized clothes are positive about the idea. They have admitted that wearing smaller-sized clothes made them feel better about themselves.

obesity can lead to other serious health problems, such as diabetes and heart disease.

Eating disorders are often the result of using food to cope with stress. When people are frustrated or unhappy about themselves, they tend to use food as a way to show they can control their lives. Some eat too much; others, too little. Eventually, for those with eating disorders, the disorder becomes the one in control.

Eating disorders can be treated successfully. It may be a long process, though. The person needs to learn healthier, positive attitudes toward food, as well as effective ways of dealing with emotional problems. It is possible to recover from an eating disorder.

2

Understanding Eating Disorders

ACTRESS JAMIE-LYNN SIGLER was only sixteen years old in August 1997 when she won the role of Meadow Soprano in *The Sopranos*, a popular HBO television series. After filming the pilot episode, Jamie-Lynn had to wait to find out whether the show would be picked up for a full season. Meanwhile, she had to deal with her own drama at home: breaking up with her high school boyfriend. Jamie-Lynn felt rejected and deeply hurt by the breakup. She became seriously depressed. She had always been hard on herself, but now she felt even more insecure. Jamie-Lynn started to question her looks and her body. Her friends talked about dieting. They told her that if she lost five

Actress Jamie-Lynn Sigler arrives at a 2007 Hollywood award show. She is now recovered from an eating disorder she had developed ten years earlier.

pounds, then her ex-boyfriend would take her back. That became the start of what eventually developed into an eating disorder.[1]

Desperate to lose weight, Jamie-Lynn became worried about every single calorie she put into her mouth. She decided she wasn't going to have dessert anymore. She also became obsessed with exercise, hoping to burn all the calories she did eat. She started exercising twenty minutes every morning before school. When she noticed that she had lost some weight, Jamie-Lynn was motivated to lose more. She decided to exercise an hour before school. She also figured it might help if she stopped eating bread.

By November, Jamie-Lynn had restricted her diet to only 500 calories a day. (The average teenage girl needs more than 2,000 calories a day to stay healthy.) For breakfast, she would eat two egg whites; for lunch she would have a scooped-out bagel and a diet soda. Her dinner consisted of a fat-free yogurt. Often she skipped meals altogether. And her one-hour morning workout turned into four hours. She even tried to fit exercise into everything she did. At school, for example, she would frequently ask to go to the bathroom so that she could burn calories by walking to and from class. When she did her laundry, she would carry one sock at a time to the laundry room. That way she would have to go up and down the stairs ten times. She even did squats while she was making her bed.

By April 1998, Jamie-Lynn, at 5 feet 6 inches tall, had gone from 120 pounds down to only 90 pounds. Her severe weight loss started to take its toll on various aspects of her life, including her health. At school, her grades had dropped because she kept falling asleep in class. She was getting sick a lot more often. Her hair was falling out. Classmates made comments like "Oh my God" and "That's disgusting!" when they saw her. Jamie-Lynn was so thin, she had to wear children's clothes. She remembers looking in the mirror, seeing her bones showing through her skin, and thinking, "I look horrible, but I can't stop this."[2] She finally realized she had a serious problem—she had anorexia.

Jamie-Lynn became really depressed. Originally, she had felt like her weight was one thing in her life she could control. But now her life seemed to be spinning out of control more than ever. She even had thoughts of suicide. That was when she decided to tell her parents that she had an eating disorder and needed help. The next day, she went to a psychiatrist. She was relieved to finally talk to someone about her feelings.

A few weeks later, a nutritionist had Jamie-Lynn make gradual changes in her eating habits, such as adding a piece of toast to her breakfast and fruit toppings to her yogurt. She also cut back on her exercising. However, treatment of her anorexia did not go smoothly. One time at a party, she ate a piece of cake. When she woke up the next morning, she was convinced that she wouldn't fit into her jeans. She immediately went to the gym and worked out for two hours. After that, she went back to the psychiatrist, who gave her a prescription for medication to calm her down.

Jamie-Lynn went to film the first season of *The Sopranos* in June 1998. It had been a year since the cast had seen her. They were shocked by her appearance. The series creator, David Chase, hardly recognized her. He became worried about her frail appearance and wondered whether she would be physically able to handle the job. This was a wake-up call for Jamie-Lynn. She did not want to lose her dream job. Determined to get well again, she started to eat more and no longer exercised every day. By the end of the season she was living a healthier lifestyle, and she was feeling good. She now eats a healthy diet, and she stops eating when she's full. She exercises no more than two to three times a week.

In 2002, Jamie-Lynn talked about her eating disorder in her book, *Wise Girl: What I've Learned About Life, Love, and Loss.*[3] She also became a spokesperson for the National Eating Disorders Association. "I went public with my eating disorder because I wanted to make some good come of this terrible episode in my life," Jamie-Lynn explains. "I want to reach young girls

Jamie-Lynn Sigler signs copies of her book, *Wise Girl: What I've Learned About Life, Love, and Loss.*

Worldwide Attention

Karen Carpenter and her brother Richard were superstar singers in the 1970s and early 1980s. Their fans were shocked when Karen died suddenly of a heart attack in 1983. The heart attack was the result of a long struggle with anorexia nervosa. Karen's death brought worldwide attention to this eating disorder.

Richard and Karen Carpenter, 1970 Grammy-Award winners.

and let them know there is a way out; there is help available. No one should have to suffer in silence."[4]

Focusing on Food

Most of the time, people eat because they are hungry. Their stomachs may rumble, alerting them that they need to eat food right away. But people do not always eat only when they are hungry. They may eat because they are bored. Munching on a bag of potato chips gives them something to do while they are watching a movie or a TV program. Or they may eat when there is something to celebrate, such as a birthday party or winning a baseball game. And sometimes people overeat or refuse to eat because they feel unhappy.

For some people, though, food is not just a part of their life—it *is* their life. They are constantly thinking about it, from the moment they wake up in the morning until they go to bed at night. When food becomes the main focus in a person's life, that person could have an eating disorder. For people with eating disorders, food becomes an obsession. Their eating habits

Justine Bateman (second from the left), pictured here with the cast of *Family Ties*, struggled with anorexia, bulimia, and compulsive overeating.

may become extreme and dangerous. They may starve themselves (anorexia nervosa), binge and purge (bulimia), or binge without purging (binge eating disorder/compulsive overeating).

The differences between anorexia, bulimia, and compulsive overeating are not always clear-cut. Some people develop more than one eating disorder, alternating between one and another. Justine Bateman, a star from the 1980s TV show *Family Ties*, suffered from all three disorders. In a 1996 interview in *TV Guide*, Justine described her decade-long struggle: "[I would make rules like] I can have one more cookie if I go throw it all up later. Or I can have this now if I skip lunch later." She was certain that people knew what she was doing. "In fact, when they'd say, 'You look anorexic,' I'd take it as a compliment," she recalls.[5] At the time, Justine could not imagine that there was such a thing as being "too thin."

> Eating disorders are not just about food. They are often a way to deal with emotions and difficult situations.

Eating disorders are not just about food, however. They are often a way to deal with emotions and difficult situations. (Justine Bateman blames the pressures of being famous during her teen years as the cause of her

Out of Control

People with eating disorders often feel like their life is out of *control*. Many mental health experts believe that control plays an important part in eating disorders. When people feel sad and miserable, they often feel like they have little or no control over their problems. People with an eating disorder use food as a tool—something they *can* control.

eating disorders.) The disordered eating behavior is considered a mental health condition that, if left untreated, can go on for months or even years. In severe cases, the condition can lead to serious health problems and even death.

Body Image

My ears are too big. I wish my hair were straight. I look fat. I'm too short. Everybody seems to have something they wish they could change about their physical appearance. People struggling with an eating disorder, however, cannot stop thinking about the way they look. They are constantly putting themselves down. Their body image—the way they see themselves and feel about their body—is very negative.

Studies have shown that many young people are unhappy with the way they look. According to the Renfrew Center Foundation for Eating Disorders in Philadelphia, about 50 percent of girls between the ages of eleven and thirteen see themselves as overweight. And 80 percent of thirteen-year-old girls have tried to lose weight by dieting.[6]

A negative body image often leads to poor self-esteem. Self-esteem is a combination of how much people value themselves, how much confidence they

ple with low self-esteem overlook their good points and concentrate on their imperfections.

> Studies have shown that many young people are unhappy with the way they look. Eighty percent of thirteen-year-old girls have tried to lose weight by dieting.

have, and how satisfied they are with themselves. People with low self-esteem do not like themselves. They overlook their good points, such as intelligence or skills, and focus on their physical imperfections. They may think that other people also focus on these imperfections. People with high self-esteem accept the way they look and like the way they are. They allow themselves to take credit for their accomplishments and aren't devastated when they fail at things in life. They just try harder next time. Such people are less likely to develop food obsessions and eating disorders.

Eating disorders typically first appear during adolescence. This is the time when people form their self-image (their identity, who they are). Adolescence is a hard time for many because the body is going through dramatic changes. These changes occur during puberty, the time in which a child develops into an adult. As puberty begins, the brain releases hormones. These chemicals produce physical changes in the body. For many girls, this means gaining weight and storing more fat in the breasts and around the hips. This is a normal part of growing up, but it can be devastating to teens who compare themselves to extremely thin movie stars and models in magazines. These celebrities seem to have the ideal body—but they do not represent the average person.

People with high self-esteem accept the way they look and like the way they are. They aren't devastated when they fail at things in life. Such people are less likely to develop food obsessions and eating disorders.

Typically, adolescents are very sensitive to the world around them and how they relate to other people. Some teens base their entire self-esteem on their body image. The way they see themselves may be distorted—that is, they see things differently, not the way they really are. For adolescents who desperately want to fit in and be accepted, being overweight in a society that says thin is beautiful makes it difficult to build self-esteem.

What Causes Eating Disorders?

What makes some people more likely than others to develop an eating disorder? Health experts are often quick to blame society for focusing too much on looks

Famous People Who Have Struggled With an Eating Disorder

Many people think that celebrities represent the ideal body type. However, even famous people can have a negative body image. Constantly being in the public eye and trying to look "perfect" can cause a great deal of pressure.

A number of celebrities have had eating disorders.

Name	Occupation	Type of Eating Disorder
Paula Abdul	Singer, dancer	Anorexia & bulimia
Kate Beckinsale	Actress	Anorexia
Victoria Beckham	Singer (Spice Girls)	Binge eating
Kelly Clarkson	Singer (American Idol)	Bulimia
Princess Diana	Princess of Wales	Bulimia
Emme	Model	Binge eating
Sally Field	Actress	Anorexia & bulimia
Calista Flockhart	Actress	Anorexia
Jane Fonda	Actress	Anorexia & bulimia

Name	Occupation	Type of Eating Disorder
Tracey Gold	Actress *(Growing Pains)*	Anorexia
Christy Henrich	Olympic gymnast	Anorexia
Felicity Huffman	Actress *(Desperate Housewives)*	Anorexia & bulimia
Janet Jackson	Singer	Binge eating
Elton John	Singer	Bulimia
Wynonna Judd	Actress	Binge eating
Katharine McPhee	Singer *(American Idol)*	Bulimia
Alanis Morissette	Singer	Anorexia & bulimia
Dennis Quaid	Actor	Anorexia
Portia de Rossi	Actress	Anorexia
Christina Ricci	Actress	Anorexia
Ashlee Simpson	Singer	Anorexia
Oprah Winfrey	Talk show host	Binge eating

and constantly sending the message that "thin is in." Actually, there is no single cause. Researchers believe that eating disorders are genetic—people inherit genes that make them more likely to develop the condition. In a 2000 study, researchers at Virginia Commonwealth University studied the genetic risk of anorexia nervosa in a sample of 2,163 female twins. They concluded that genetics increased the chances of getting an eating disorder by an estimated 58 percent. The findings were published in the *American Journal of Psychiatry.*[7] However, other factors are most likely involved as well. For example, the pressure to be thin could be a trigger that leads to an eating disorder in people who have inherited genes that increase their risk.

According to the National Eating Disorders Association, eating disorders are caused by a combination of factors. They may include the following:

Psychological:
- Low self-esteem
- Feeling a lack of control in life
- Depression, anxiety, anger, or loneliness

Interpersonal:
- Troubled family and personal relationships
- Difficulty expressing emotions and feelings

- History of being teased about size and weight

- History of physical or sexual abuse

Social:

- Social pressures that put too much importance on being thin and having the "perfect body"

- Beauty defined according to body weights and shapes that most people do not have

- Society valuing people based on physical appearance rather than inner qualities and strengths

Biological:

- Eating disorders often run in families. Researchers have found that certain genes may be involved in the development of eating disorders.

- Researchers believe that chemical imbalances in the brain play a role in eating disorders.

Family Life

In the 1870s, French psychiatrist Ernest-Charles Lasègue suggested that pressures at home played an important role in the development of anorexia nervosa. By the mid-1980s, therapists who had treated anorexic patients found that there may be some truth to this observation. During therapy sessions, many anorexic patients described their mothers as anxious, overprotective perfectionists, who often controlled various aspects of their life. Fathers were described as moody, withdrawn, and passive. In general, anorexic patients had trouble developing their own identity and separating themselves from the family. In many cases, their families had trouble dealing with conflict.

Researchers have not been able to prove a link between the personalities of patients' parents and eating disorders. However, modern studies have shown that many patients have a troubling home environment. Typically, the families tend to use eating or refusing food as ways to feel better. Thoughtless comments like, "No second helping for you! Your hips are too big already." may make kids focus too much on food. A mother who is constantly dieting or a father who no longer eats meat and potatoes and worries constantly about heart disease can also help a child to develop negative attitudes toward eating. Parents who eat moderate portions of nutritious foods and lead an active life, on the other hand, can be positive role models. Their children may be less likely to develop eating disorders.

3

What Is Anorexia?

IN THE SUMMER OF 2004, Tyler Brown was a healthy nine year old, weighing 49 pounds (22 kg). He had always been a picky eater, but his parents became really worried when the only thing he would eat was a carrot covered with peanut butter. Within three months, Tyler looked very thin and weak—he was down to only 39 pounds (17.7 kg). His parents took him to their family doctor, who recommended that Tyler get treatment at an eating disorders clinic for anorexia nervosa.

It took some time before Tyler's family and their doctor finally found an eating disorders clinic that would accept a (by then) ten-year-old boy. Tyler was barely conscious by the time they arrived at Children's

Hospital in Omaha, Nebraska, hundreds of miles from their home in Illinois. During his stay at the clinic, Tyler talked about his issues with food. He revealed that he was afraid of getting fat. He was certain that eating food would make him fat, so he continued to restrict his diet until he was barely eating anything at all. The program helped Tyler deal with his worries about gaining weight. He admits, though, that he still gets nervous when he notices he has outgrown a pair of jeans, but he doesn't let it control his life anymore.[1]

> The medical name *anorexia nervosa* is used to describe an eating disorder characterized by severe weight loss due to self-starvation.

A Loss of Appetite

Anorexia means "loss of appetite." Doctors often use this term as a symptom for such diseases as cancer or AIDS, in which weight loss is a common problem. But in these cases, they are not talking about an eating disorder. The medical name *anorexia nervosa* is used to describe an eating disorder characterized by severe weight loss due to self-starvation. Many people call it anorexia for short. The word *anorexic* is often used to describe someone who is extremely thin.

People with anorexia nervosa may not have lost their appetite as its name suggests. In fact, they may feel hungry, but their fear of gaining weight is so intense that they choose to ignore their hunger pangs. (In late stages of starvation, people may no longer feel hungry at all.)

What Is Appetite?

Appetite is the urge to eat. Its main job is to get you to eat when your body's food supply is getting low and needs to be restocked. Hunger pangs are the brain's way of letting you know that you are hungry. Appetite may be activated when you feel absolutely stuffed after a big meal, and yet you can still find a little room for dessert. An unpleasant experience or an illness can "turn off" appetite even when the body is hungry.

A part of the brain called the hypothalamus contains a number of control centers. These centers send messages to various parts of the body to regulate important body processes. Some of these centers control strong emotions such as anger, fear, and pleasure. There are also two different centers that play major roles in appetite. The *hunger center* sends signals telling you to eat. The *satiety center* signals that you have had enough to eat, and so you feel "full."

What Are Calories?

People who are trying to lose weight often count calories. Calories are units of energy stored in food. They give you the energy to do your everyday activities—breathing, walking, thinking, sleeping, playing ball. Carbohydrates, proteins, and fats contain calories. Fats can store more than twice as much energy as proteins or carbohydrates. One gram of fat contains about 9 calories of energy. One gram of protein or carbohydrate contains only 4 calories. When people eat more calories than their bodies need, the extra fuel gets stored as fat.

How many calories do you need every day? That depends on your age, gender, and activity level. Do you play sports or do you spend a lot of time sitting in front of the computer? The more active you are, the more calories you will burn. The more energy you use, the more calories you need to eat. On the average, a teenage girl needs about 1,800 to 2,400 calories a day to be healthy, and a teenage boy needs about 2,200 to 3,000.[2] Teens who eat less than 1,600 calories a day are not getting enough nutrients, which can lead to health problems.[3]

Eating Rituals

Many people with eating disorders suffer from obsessive-compulsive disorder (OCD). They develop rituals—things they do every day, often several times a day. They are trying to bring a feeling of order and control into their lives. A common ritual for people with OCD is washing their hands a certain number of times and at certain times of the day.

For people with eating disorders, OCD rituals often revolve around food. In anorexia, people may eat foods in a certain order, rearrange food on their plate, or chew a piece of food for ten minutes before swallowing it. These rituals may become very unusual and strict. For example, a girl with anorexia may cut up the solid foods into tiny pieces. She may put the controlled portions in small containers and line them neatly in rows. Foods may have to be separate on the plate, not touching.

People with OCD cannot control their behavior. Their obsessions—about food or about being thin—may cause them to spend hours each day performing their rituals. They need professional help.

People with anorexia may fast, that is, go through periods of eating nothing at all. When they do eat, they restrict (reduce) the amount of food they eat. They don't take in enough calories or nutrients to stay

People with anorexia typically weigh themselves many times a day. They see themselves as fat no matter how much weight they lose.

healthy. Some anorexics lose weight by exercising excessively. Exercise is a very effective way to burn calories. However, anorexia can become a prob-

> People with anorexia are literally starving themselves. In fact, as many as 10 percent of anorexia nervosa patients die.

lem among some athletes, who exercise to an extreme. Studies have shown that ballet dancers, gymnasts, and long-distance runners have a higher-than-average risk of developing anorexia.

People with anorexia are obsessed with their weight. They typically weigh themselves several times a day. No matter how much weight they lose, it never seems to be enough. When they look in the mirror, they may complain about their big hips, big thighs, or bulging stomach. While they see themselves as terribly overweight, however, they often look frighteningly thin to the rest of world.

Dying to Be Thin

People with anorexia are literally starving themselves. They are not getting all the nutrients their body needs to stay healthy. As a result, anorexia can cause a number of health problems. In some cases, it can even lead to death. In fact, as many as 10 percent of anorexia nervosa

Holy Starvation

Anorexia has been around for centuries. In ancient Rome, some wealthy Roman women of the Christian faith showed their devotion to God by refusing to eat and going through long periods of starvation, called fasts. One actually starved to death in A.D. 383—the first recorded death from anorexia.

Saint Catherine of Siena

During the Middle Ages and early Renaissance, particularly between 1200 and 1600, some highly religious Christian women also practiced fasting. The Catholic Church officially declared a few of them to be holy saints. People were amazed by their "miraculous" ability to survive for so long without food. Saint Catherine of Siena (1347–1380), for example, was constantly struggling for spiritual perfection. She felt shame because she was having "impure thoughts." Catherine wanted to prove her loyalty to Christ by restricting her diet to only a handful of herbs every day. If she was forced to eat, she pushed twigs down her throat to make herself vomit. Years of starvation led to her death at the age of thirty-three.

patients die.[4] This is the highest death rate of any mental illness.

Here are some of the effects anorexia can have on different parts of the body:

Wasting away. When the body is starved of food, it starts burning its fat stores for energy. When all the fat reserves are used up, the body burns muscle. The muscles become weak and tired. Eventually the body feeds on its own organs.

Heart. Without good nutrition, the heart does not have enough energy to pump blood effectively. The heart muscle gets thinner. Patients feel weak and have trouble keeping  warm. They may develop low blood pressure, slow heart rate, fluttering of the heart (palpitations), or even heart failure.

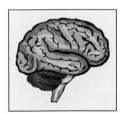 Brain. Patients may become light-headed and have problems thinking clearly. Kids may have trouble learning in school. Structures in the brain are changed. Some of these changes are permanent. In some patients, the brain actually shrinks, causing personality changes. In addition, depression and irritability are common in people with eating disorders.

Lack of electrolytes. Electrolytes are salts and minerals, such as potassium, sodium, and magnesium, that the body needs to stay healthy. An imbalance of electrolytes can cause a buildup of body fluids, resulting in swollen legs and ankles. Dehydration (serious water loss) may also occur. Signs of dehydration include dry mouth, decreased urine, sunken eyes, and dizziness.

 **Kidneys.** A serious loss of fluids can lead to kidney stones or kidney failure.

Digestion. The digestive tract slows down, making patients feel constipated and full.

Hair and nails. A lack of protein in the diet causes hair to become thin, dry, and brittle. Nails become brittle and break easily.

Skin. Skin gets dry and tends to crack. In some patients, the skin turns yellow as a result of liver damage.

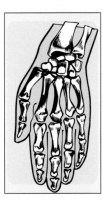 **Bones.** Anorexic kids do not get enough calcium, a nutrient that is necessary for building strong bones, especially during the growing years. Their bodies also stop producing hormones that are needed to grow and strengthen bones. Their bones become thinner. Later in life, they may develop osteoporosis, a condition in

which bones are weak and break easily. The longer anorexia continues, the weaker the bones become; the bones may never be strong again.

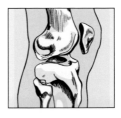

Hormones. Serious weight loss can keep the body from producing sex hormones, which can delay puberty in both boys and girls. Kids may have problems growing. Getting too thin after a girl starts her monthly menstrual periods may cause her to stop having periods. Amenorrhea (lack of menstrual periods) is common among girls with anorexia. Girls who continue to be anorexic as adults may have trouble getting pregnant. Boys will not develop strong muscles and may not grow as tall as they could have.

A Brain Connection

Studies have shown that anorexia and bulimia may be linked to changes in the amount of serotonin in the brain. Serotonin is a neurotransmitter that controls hunger, sleep, impulse control, anger, depression, anxiety, and perception. Neurotransmitters are chemicals that carry messages from one part of the brain to another. Too much or too little serotonin in the brain can cause mixed signals, which can affect a person's way of thinking and behaving.

Researchers have theories about serotonin's role in eating disorders. A low level of serotonin may lead to depression, which may then result in anorexia or bulimia. (Depression may also be a side effect of eating disorders.) Bingeing on sweets, starches, and carbohydrates increases serotonin, which actually helps the person feel better for a while. It produces a temporary state of well-being. On the other hand, too much serotonin may lead to constant anxiety. Starvation lowers the serotonin level, making the person feel calm and back in control. Severely limiting food intake and bingeing (with or without purging) can lead to an imbalance of serotonin levels.

4

What Is Bulimia?

GROWING UP, JULIE tried hard to be the best at everything she did. She was one of the top players on her soccer team. She got excellent grades. She was very popular in school. Her parents expected nothing less. But Julie was tired of being "perfect" all the time. No matter what she did, she never felt she was good enough.

In her mind, Julie always thought that beauty meant being thin. Her mother was thin and beautiful. In the seventh grade, Julie became overweight and really hated her body. A number of times her mother made comments to her about her weight problem. Julie felt like her mother was constantly criticizing her.

At the start of eighth grade, Julie was spending time

with a friend who was anorexic. She felt bad about what her friend was doing to her body, but at the same time, she admired her for her ability to do it.

In November, Julie's parents wanted Julie to be tested academically. With her high test scores, she jumped up to eleventh grade. She was only fourteen, and she sat in a classroom with seventeen year olds. She became so overwhelmed with pressure that she soon gained another ten pounds. That was when she vowed to lose weight. One day after eating, Julie went straight for the bathroom and made herself throw up by pushing her fingers down her throat. For the first time, she felt like she had control over something.

Two weeks later, Julie's parents found out about her vomiting after meals. "We're so disappointed," they told her. "You have to snap out of it!"[1] She felt so alone at that moment. She knew she couldn't stop even if she tried. Julie was very stressed out trying to meet everybody's expectations.

Soon Julie started purging five times a day. She did it anywhere she could—at home, school, clubs, parties. She would turn on the water faucet to hide what she was doing. Afterward, she would wash her face and chew gum to cover her bad breath. The acid in her vomit damaged her teeth. She also developed scarring on her knuckle from constantly sticking her finger down her throat.

Not knowing what else to do, Julie's parents took her to a psychiatrist, who prescribed antidepressants for her. After a few days, Julie stopped taking the medicine because it was making her feel more anxious than before. At this point, her bingeing and purging seemed to be controlling her, not the other way around. She fell into deep depression. She even had thoughts of killing herself.

In March, Julie did try to kill herself, but fortunately her mother found her in time. Julie cried, telling her mother that she felt like a failure, and that she couldn't handle life anymore. She told her mother she wanted to get better and was willing to get help. Her parents took her to an eating disorders clinic at Stanford University in California for treatment of bulimia. The doctors there used scare tactics, telling Julie what horrible things she was doing to her body by bingeing and purging. Her hair was thinning. Her throat was bleeding. And she was at risk for having a heart attack. For a while the treatment worked—she stopped purging completely.

In the fall, Julie had to repeat her junior year of high

school. Meanwhile, she continued to see a therapist. It wasn't long, though, before she started putting tremendous pressure on herself again. Within two months, Julie was making herself vomit again. "Every time I purged," she recalled, "I hated myself, feeling so ashamed and alone."[2]

Julie became so depressed, she tried to kill herself again. Her mother took her to the hospital. Not long after her attempted suicide, Julie, by this time sixteen, was taken to The Center, an eating disorders clinic in Washington. The therapists there were very caring and understanding. Julie felt comfortable with them and was able to talk about her problems. She finally realized that losing weight was not going to give her a feeling of self-worth.

Gradually, Julie stopped purging. She learned how to eat a healthier diet. She took vitamins and started exercising. Therapy had made her realize that her problem was not about wanting to be thin—it was about loving herself. There are days, she admits, that she is hard on herself. But most of the time, she feels okay with who she is. She knows nobody's perfect.[3]

Bingeing and Purging

Unlike anorexia, people with bulimia (short for *bulimia nervosa*) do not avoid food. In fact, they do eat, and sometimes far more than the average person. They may "pig out" (binge) on cakes, pizzas, burgers, and other high-fat foods—taking in anywhere from 1,000 to as many as 30,000 calories in just one sitting.[4] To get rid

---

Unlike anorexia, people with bulimia do not avoid food. In fact, they do eat, and sometimes far more than the average person. To get rid of the calories, they may use various ways of purging.

---

of the calories, they may use various ways of purging: They may make themselves vomit by sticking their fingers down their throat. They may take ipecac syrup, a medicine to make them throw up. They may take laxatives or diuretics to make them go to the bathroom. (Laxatives are medicines that speed up the movement of food through the digestive system, causing a bowel movement. Diuretics are medicines that make the body produce more urine. They don't get rid of calories, but they do lower body weight by getting rid of water.)

People with bulimia may go through periods of

Exercise Bulimia

Health experts often talk about how good exercise is for the body. However, people who suffer from exercise bulimia have taken a good thing too far. In exercise bulimia, people purge what they have eaten —not by vomiting, but by exercising. They keep track of the calories they eat, and then make sure they exercise enough to burn it all off, and sometimes more.

If exercise is supposed to be good for you, then what is wrong with exercise bulimia? What happens is that exercise becomes an obsession. The workouts become excessive—far more than what experts recommend for good health. People with exercise bulimia may exercise for at least three or four hours every day, sometimes more. Exercise becomes like a drug—it is all they can think about. It may even interfere with their daily life, including their job, school, or hanging out with friends. Even worse, too much exercise can cause health problems, including injuries (such as broken bones, strains, and sprains), dehydration, exhaustion, and serious weight loss. For some bulimics, exercise is such a big part of their lives that if they miss a day, they may become anxious and depressed.

hardly eating anything at all (fasting) to "make up for" bingeing. Some bulimics burn off calories by overexercising after bingeing. This form of purging is known as exercise bulimia.

Many people with bulimia have had a history of anorexia, and about 50 percent of anorexics sometimes binge and purge.[5] As with anorexia, bulimia may be a

Feeling Blue

Depression is a common problem in people with eating disorders, especially bulimia. It is more than feeling sad or down in the dumps once in a while. Depression is a medical condition that involves feelings of sadness, despair, and hopelessness that do not go away. It affects a person's thoughts, behavior, and mood. For people with eating disorders, depression makes them feel even worse about how they see themselves and how they think others see them. People who are depressed can no longer enjoy activities the way they used to. They have very little energy to do anything, even get out of bed. They may become irritable and moody all the time. Relationships with friends and family may start to fall apart. But there are a variety of medications and therapies that can help people with depression.

> Some bulimics burn off calories by overexercising after bingeing. This form of purging is known as exercise bulimia.

way some people deal with society's pressures to be thin. They believe that the image they see in the mirror does not match the accepted ideal of beauty. As a result, they become obsessed with their weight and shape. No matter how many times they binge and purge, though, they are never happy with the way they look.

People with bulimia typically feel shame and disgust because they are embarrassed by their bulimic behavior. Following a binge, they often feel guilty and helpless. Yet they cannot stop what they are doing. Their self-esteem is seriously low, and they may become depressed. Actually, depression and anxiety are common problems in people with bulimia. In severe cases, their depression may lead to thoughts or attempts of suicide. In addition, people with bulimia are more likely to abuse alcohol and use illegal drugs than those without bulimia.

Bulimia is not easy to recognize. Many people with bulimia are not severely underweight like those with anorexia. In fact, most of them are of average weight. They are also very secretive—they will do anything they can to hide their condition from everyone. They may sneak away to binge on a "secret stash" of

People with bulimia may keep a "secret stash" of candy or other junk foods hidden in their home.

People with bulimia may look healthy on the outside, but they are doing a great deal of harm on the inside.

cookies and candies they have hidden in their bedroom. Then afterward, they lock themselves in the bathroom and throw up the food they have just eaten. They use little tricks to cover up what they have done, such as running the water faucet or taking a shower while they vomit. They may freshen their breath with a mint or chewing gum. People with bulimia do not always purge only after big binges. Sometimes they feel the need to purge after small or average-size meals. Eating particular foods, such as pizza, candy, or junk food, may also prompt an urge to purge.

What Harm Can Bulimia Do?

People with bulimia may look healthy on the outside, but they are doing a great deal of harm on the inside. Every time they purge, they are getting rid of important nutrients and fluids their body needs to stay healthy. The food that they ate never had a chance to be fully digested and absorbed into the body. Frequent purging can lead to a number of harmful effects on the body. They may include the following:

Heart. A lack of good nutrition (due to frequent

purging) may cause heart problems such as irregular heartbeat, low blood pressure, or even heart failure. Overuse of ipecac syrup may damage the heart muscle and cause a fast or irregular heartbeat.

Brain. A lack of nutrients may damage the brain. This can make it difficult to concentrate and think clearly.

Digestive system. Vomiting sends stomach acid up through the esophagus and into the mouth. Frequent vomiting may cause acid burns or tears inside the esophagus. It can also lead to stomach pain and ulcers (sores in the stomach lining). In rare cases, binge eating may cause a tear in the stomach. Overuse of laxatives leads to a number of digestion problems, including constipation, irregular bowel movements, bloating, diarrhea, and abdominal cramps.

Lack of electrolytes. The electrolytes important for good health (potassium, sodium, and magnesium) do not get absorbed into the body if a person purges. Without the right amount of electrolytes, people feel tired and weak. In addition, important organs, including the heart and the colon, may not work effectively. A lack of potassium, which helps control the work of the heart, can be especially dangerous.

Dehydration. Dehydration occurs when the body loses large amounts of fluids due to frequent vomiting, excessive diarrhea (by overuse of laxatives), or frequent urination (by overuse of diuretics). It can also occur if the person does not replace fluids (by drinking water) after exercising excessively. (Sweating during exercise removes fluids from the body.) Signs of dehydration include dry mouth, decreased urine, sunken eyes, blurry vision, dizziness, and fainting.

Teeth and gums. Strong stomach acids in vomit can cause teeth to decay and form cavities. Sores may also develop on the gums.

Throat and mouth. Frequent vomiting can cause a sore throat and hoarse voice. Sores develop in the mouth. Blood in the vomit indicates severe damage to the throat.

Cheeks. Frequent vomiting may cause "chipmunk cheeks," caused by swollen salivary glands in the cheeks.

Skin. Skin may be dry due to a lack of fluids. Cuts or scars may develop on the knuckles from sticking fingers down the throat.

Hormones. The body may not produce enough of the sex hormone estrogen. Females may have irregular or missed monthly menstrual periods, and males and females may develop osteoporosis.

Chemicals in the Brain

As discussed earlier, studies have shown that low levels of the neurotransmitter serotonin have been linked to cases of anorexia, as well as bulimia. Other studies have found that some people with bulimia also have a reduced supply of the hormone cholecystokinin (CCK). CCK is normally released by cells in the intestines after a meal. As the hormone passes into the blood, it signals the satiety center in the hypothalamus. The larger the meal, the more CCK is produced; at a certain level, you feel "full."

In people with bulimia, the CCK level is lower than normal, even after a meal. So the appetite-reducing mechanism is not turned on, and the person continues to eat. Researchers have found that when bulimics are given CCK, most of them stop or at least cut back on their binges. Follow-up studies are looking at the effects of CCK on people with bulimia. Researchers hope that their findings may lead to an effective treatment for the condition.

5

What Is Binge Eating Disorder?

ALISON SPINELLI HAS had problems with her weight almost her whole life. When she was in second grade, she got up to 100 pounds (45 kg). Kids in her class were often cruel, making fun of her large size. Their jokes only got worse when Alison couldn't play on the swings during recess because she was too big for them. In class, she had to sit on the floor for a week until they could find a larger desk for her. In third grade, Alison gained another 60 pounds (27 kg). She continued to feel sad and lonely, as her classmates taunted and teased her. Her mother, Donna, recalled Alison crying all afternoon one day, after being teased at a classmate's birthday party. After Alison finished crying, she started eating. She ate huge amounts of food.

She just couldn't stop herself. "Food was everything to me," Alison said. "If anyone said something that made me emotional, I would cry, feel frustrated, and eat."[1]

By age twelve, Alison weighed 292 pounds (132 kg). Donna tried to get her daughter to cut back her snacking on chips, cookies, and ice cream. But then Alison would get angry, telling her mother, "You don't love me!"[2]

Alison's obsession with food was affecting everyone in the family. She would get upset very easily. Her sister, Jennifer, tried to be sensitive to her feelings, but soon it was just too difficult to be around her. Finally, Alison's parents decided to get help for their daughter. They took her to Camp Kingsmont, a retreat for overweight kids in West Stockbridge, Massachusetts. The camp counselors all used to be overweight themselves. They taught the kids about nutrition, exercise, and self-esteem. At first Alison was angry with her parents for making her go, but then she started to feel good about being there. She liked being around people who knew what she was going through. She also learned a lot. "Camp changed the way I look at food and portion control," she said.[3] Her new eating habits, which began to include salads and vegetables, as well as an exercise

A Healthy Appetite

Children and teenagers may sometimes eat a lot, but that doesn't necessarily mean they have binge eating disorder. Kids can have big appetites, especially when they are going through growth spurts. They can grow several inches in a single year, so they need extra nutrients to fuel their growing bodies. Active kids may also eat a lot because their bodies are burning off extra calories.

program, helped her lose 30 pounds (14 kg). When she went back to the camp the following summer, she lost another 37 pounds (17 kg). Gradually, she has been getting the weight off. She feels much better about herself. She is happy about the progress she has made and hopes it continues.[4]

Health experts say that obesity—being seriously overweight—is becoming increasingly common among young people. Alison is one of millions of American children who is overweight or obese. And many of them continue to be overweight into adulthood.

Many people who have binge eating disorder are overweight or obese. Binge eating disorder is often considered the third main eating disorder after anorexia and bulimia, even though, as of 2007, it was not officially recognized by the American Psychiatric Association. That could soon change. In February 2007, the McLean Hospital, an affiliate of Harvard Medical School, reported surprising findings in the first national survey of people with eating disorders. Researchers found that binge eating disorder was *more* common than either anorexia or bulimia. In the survey of more than 9,000 people across the United States, 0.9 percent of women and 0.3 percent of men reported having anorexia at some point in their lives; 1.5 percent of women and 0.5 percent of men reported having bulimia; and binge eating disorder affected 3.5 percent of women and 2 percent of men.[5]

Eating Too Much

Everybody overeats once in a while. With binge eating disorder, however, people eat enormous amounts of food on a fairly regular basis. Afraid of what people might say about their eating habits, binge eaters may gather food and go somewhere private so that they can eat by themselves. They often eat really fast, and they keep on eating even after they are no longer hungry. They feel completely out of control while they are binge eating. They cannot stop no matter how hard they try. That is why binge eating disorder is often called compulsive overeating. Binge eaters see food as comfort when they are feeling stressed, upset, hurt, or angry. They feel better while they are eating, but after the binge, they start to feel sad and guilty. As in other eating disorders, depression is common among people with binge eating disorder.

Binge eating disorder sounds a lot like bulimia: They both involve eating excessive amounts of food, losing control while eating, and feeling guilt or shame afterward. However, they do have one important difference: People with binge eating disorder do not purge what they have eaten, as people with bulimia do. That is why many people with binge eating disorder are overweight. Eating too much too often may lead to obesity, which can cause serious health problems, such as heart disease, type 2 diabetes, and cancer. However, it is important to note that not every binge eater is obese, and not everyone who is obese is a binge eater.

What Does Overweight Mean?

Overweight means having an unhealthy amount of body fat. Everybody has some body fat, which can be very useful. In addition to storing energy, it gives the body cushioning and insulation from the cold. It protects the organs, and in girls a certain extra amount of body fat is needed for a healthy reproductive system. However, too much body fat can harm a person's health and make it more difficult to move around.

People become overweight when they get more calories (from foods and drinks) than their bodies use. This can happen when they overeat, taking in huge numbers of calories. People may also gain weight when they are inactive. Physical activity, such as riding a bike or playing soccer, uses more calories than riding in a car or reading a book. Any extra calories are stored in fat cells found in certain parts of the body, especially the waist, thighs, and buttocks. Too much stored fat can make a person overweight.

Health experts are worried about the rising rates of obesity in the United States. The government-sponsored National Health and Nutrition Examination Survey (NHANES) for 2003–2004 indicated that about 66 percent of U.S. adults, ages 20 and over, were either overweight or obese.[7] This figure is much higher than the 56 percent found in the NHANES report for 1988–1994.[8] These surveys also showed that American

What is BMI?

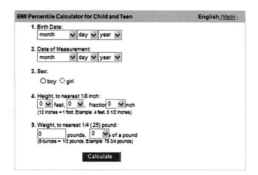

How do you know if you are overweight, underweight, or at an ideal weight? Health experts use a scale called body mass index, or BMI, to estimate how much body fat a person has.

The BMI is calculated from a person's height and weight, according to this formula:

$$\text{Weight (pounds)}/[\text{Height (inches)}]^2 \times 703 \ \textit{or}$$

$$\text{Weight (kg)}/[\text{Height (m)}]^2$$

People who are overweight generally have too much body weight for their height. The U.S. Centers for Disease Control and Prevention (CDC) and World Health Organization (WHO) use the following chart to determine how healthy a person's weight is:

BMI Ranges for Adults[6]:

BMI	Weight Status
Below 18.5	Underweight
18.5–24.9	Normal
25.0–29.0	Overweight
30.0 and Above	Obese

These BMI ranges are fairly accurate for young adults, especially those around 18 to 20 years old. It doesn't work for children, though. During an annual physical checkup, doctors calculate their BMI and then to compare it to standard charts for boys and girls ages 2 to 19. The result is expressed in a percentile, which shows how they rank in the child population. A child with a BMI greater than the 85th percentile (that is, heavier than 85 percent of children of the same age and gender) is considered at risk of overweight. Children with a BMI greater than the 95th percentile are considered obese.

Health experts believe that the BMI can give misleading results for some adults. For example, athletes can have a high BMI, but that doesn't mean that they are overweight. Muscle weighs more than fat, so a healthy athlete may have a high BMI in spite of a very low amount of body fat. The simple BMI equation also does not consider sex differences, although healthy women usually have more body fat than healthy men of the same height. The BMI does not reflect changes with age and differences between people of different races, nationalities, and ethnic groups. So it is really only a rough guide.

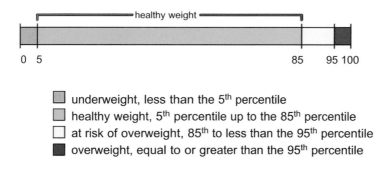

Physical activity burns calories that may otherwise be stored in fat cells.

children and teenagers have been getting heavier, too. According to the 2003–2004 NHANES report, about 17.1 percent of U.S. children and teenagers (ages 2 to 19) were overweight,[9] compared to about 11 percent in 1988-1994.[10]

The Dangers of Binge Eating

The weight problem that is often linked with binge eating disorder can have many harmful effects on the body. Carrying around a lot of excess weight puts a strain on the body. Overweight people often lack energy and feel tired. They may have trouble sleeping comfortably at night. Other more serious health problems may also develop. They may include:

Type 2 diabetes. As the obesity rate increases, so does the number of children with type 2 diabetes. Diabetes is a condition in which the body cannot store and use sugar properly, resulting in unusually high amounts of sugar in the blood. Type 2 diabetes is often linked with obesity.

High blood pressure. Overweight people are more likely to develop high blood pressure because their heart has to work harder to pump blood around the body. High blood pressure is a risk factor for heart disease.

High blood cholesterol levels. People who have extra body fat often have high blood cholesterol levels. Cholesterol is an important fatty substance needed for a healthy body. But too much of it may clog up arteries, making it harder for blood to flow through the body. High cholesterol is a risk factor for heart disease.

Heart disease. Heart disease may develop after years of strain on the heart due to certain risk factors, including obesity, high blood pressure, and high blood cholesterol level.

Lung problems. Obesity can interfere with the work of the lungs. It becomes harder to breathe and to keep up with others in running and other physical activities.

Cancer. Obesity increases the risk of developing certain kinds of cancers, such as those affecting the colon, kidney, or prostate.

Osteoarthritis. Excessive body weight damages the cartilage and joints by putting extra strain on the joints.

Liver disease. Obesity can cause fatty deposits in the liver, scarring, and liver failure.

Gallbladder disease. Obese people have an increased risk of developing gallstones. Gallstones are small, hard, painful, pebble-like objects that form in the gallbladder. They are made mostly of cholesterol and calcium salts.

6

Diagnosis and Treatment

WHEN TWENTY-TWO-year-old Katharine McPhee became runner-up on the *American Idol* TV show in May 2006, she felt as though she had won the singing competition. "*American Idol*," Katharine says, "saved my life."[1] She meant that literally. Katharine had been struggling with bulimia when she auditioned for *American Idol* in August the previous year. At that time, her eating disorder was getting so out of control that she was throwing up as many as seven times a day. When Katharine realized how this was harming her vocal cords, she finally decided to get help.

Growing up in Los Angeles, Katharine was always concerned about her body. She spent much of her childhood going to dance classes and looking at herself

American Idol contestant Katharine McPhee decided to seek treatment for her bulimia. The disease was harming her vocal cords.

in a room full of mirrors. There were times when she exercised compulsively to stay thin, and other times she didn't eat at all. In her junior year of high school, Katharine started to binge and purge. "Food was my crutch," she says. "It was how I dealt with emotions and uncomfortable situations. As soon as I would feel something, I would eat over it so that I didn't have to feel anything I didn't want to. It was literally a drug . . . nothing else mattered but getting to that food."[2] She could not eat just one slice of pizza, she had to have the *whole* pizza.

For the next five or six months, Katharine hid her bulimia. Then she decided to tell her mother about what she was doing. She was surprised at how supportive her mom was. The next day, her mom researched bulimia and wanted Katharine to go to an eating disorders treatment program. Katharine did not want to go. She told her mother that she wasn't that sick, and that she could handle it.

Later Katharine agreed to see a therapist and a dietitian. For a while, she was doing okay, but then she started to binge and purge again. She decided to go to Food Addicts Anonymous (FAA). There she could have only three meals a day and no snacks. She was also not allowed to eat anything with sugar or flour—foods FAA believes are addictive. After two weeks on the program, Katharine couldn't take it anymore. She started to binge on whatever food she could find.

It wasn't until after Katharine successfully auditioned for *American Idol* in August 2005 that she became determined to get back in control of her life. She did not want to let bulimia ruin her chances of becoming the next American Idol. In October, with the support of her parents and her boyfriend, she went for treatment at the Eating Disorder Center of California in Los Angeles. She spent three months there undergoing group and individual therapy, six days a week. "I'm really proud of her for talking about it, because there doesn't have to be a stigma," says Carolyn Costin, the center's founder and executive director. "It's a real illness, and you can get real treatment."[3]

Katharine has learned new ways of looking at food. At the center, she learned about an approach called intuitive eating, in which she realized that not allowing herself to eat "bad" foods only led to cravings for them. (That was what happened when she tried the Food Addicts Anonymous program.) On the other hand, having these foods more often, according to the intuitive eating plan, will eventually make them less desirable. Katharine had a weakness for Snickers bars, so during treatment, she had four mini-Snickers bars with each meal. Soon Katharine no longer had cravings to eat Snickers bars.

During *American Idol,* Katharine continued to talk to a therapist every week, and she never had a setback. She has learned how to deal with her emotions directly rather than through food. Although she does not consider herself completely healed, she is much happier

> Many people with eating disorders do not recognize, or admit, that they have a problem. As a result, they may refuse to get help.

about the way she looks. She knows that it will continue to be an ongoing battle, but at least her eating disorder is no longer taking over her life.[4]

Recognizing the Problem

Many people with eating disorders do not recognize, or admit, that they have a problem. As a result, they may refuse to get help. Friends, family members, teachers, and physicians all play an important role in helping them begin and stay with a treatment program. These people need to be encouraging, caring, and persistent.

Eating Disorders Checklist

Some Warning Signs and Symptoms	Anorexia Nervosa	Bulimia Nervosa	Binge Eating Disorder
Negative body image	✓	✓	✓
Severe weight loss in short period of time	✓		
Belief that body is overweight, even though it is actually severely underweight	✓		
Loss of monthly menstrual periods	✓	✓	
Strange eating rituals	✓		
Skipping meals	✓	✓	✓
Eating in secret	✓	✓	✓
Obsession with exercise	✓	✓	
Serious depression	✓	✓	✓
Eating large amounts of food (bingeing)		✓	✓
Self-induced vomiting, or overuse of laxatives or diuretics		✓	
Feelings of self-disgust and shame after eating	✓	✓	✓
Gaining excessive weight			✓
Abuse of alcohol and/or illegal drugs		✓	✓

They also need to be armed with information about eating disorders and their dangers. Their job is to convince the person to get help, stick with treatment, or try again.

The sooner the patient gets treatment, the better. By the time unhealthy eating patterns have become well established, they are more difficult to change. In addition, eating disorders can cause harmful effects on the

The sooner the patient gets treatment, the better. By the time unhealthy eating patterns have become well established, they are more difficult to change.

body, which should be detected and treated as soon as possible. Depression and suicide are also serious concerns.

Getting Help

Where should people go to get help? They can go to their family doctor or to a mental health professional, such as a psychiatrist or psychologist, to get a proper diagnosis. Unlike many other medical conditions, eating disorders cannot be identified by a blood test or other laboratory tests. However, these tests, along with a

Hair Test

In October 2006, researchers at Brigham Young University in Utah announced that they had developed a test that could help diagnose eating disorders by studying a patient's hair. Lead researcher Kent Hatch and his colleagues examined five strands of hair from twenty women diagnosed with anorexia and/or bulimia. The researchers compared the results to hairs taken from twenty-three women at Brigham Young University who did not have an eating disorder.

The research team tested for carbon and nitrogen levels in the hair samples. These chemicals, they say, record a kind of "diary" of a person's current diet. After analyzing the hair samples of both groups, they found that the test was 80 percent accurate in identifying women with anorexia and bulimia. Some health experts say the hair test could help confirm a diagnosis, but it should not be used alone to diagnose an eating disorder.[5]

routine physical exam, are helpful in determining whether the patient's unhealthy eating habits have damaged the body.

During the physical exam, the health professional will check the patient's weight and height and compare them to standard growth charts. Taking the person's pulse and blood pressure can show how well the heart is working. Blood tests can check for unhealthy levels of hormones, proteins, electrolytes, vitamins, and other substances, which can affect various organs of the body, such as the liver, kidneys, thyroid, and pituitary gland. The exam will also include listening to the patient's heart and lungs with a stethoscope, checking muscle strength and nerve reflexes, and feeling the outlines of organs in the abdomen.

Although all this information is useful, eating disorders are generally diagnosed mostly by collecting information about the patient's eating habits and medical history, as well as observations from family members and friends. There are also a number of questionnaires available for people with eating disorders that are very helpful in diagnosis and treatment.

The diagnosis is based on specific guidelines provided by the American Psychiatric Association. Using these guidelines, health professionals can identify the eating disorders and determine how severe the problem is. Some of the main characteristics that help to make a diagnosis include the following:

Anorexia nervosa:

- Weighs at least 15 percent below what is considered healthy compared to others of the same height, age, and gender

- Female (of childbearing age) misses at least three menstrual periods in a row
- Intense fear of gaining weight
- Belief that he or she is overweight even though he or she is severely underweight

Bulimia nervosa:

- Binges and purges at least two times a week on average, for at least three months
- Has no control over binge eating
- Appears to be obsessed with his or her body shape and weight

Binge eating disorder:

- At least two episodes of binge eating a week on average, for six months
- Has no control over binge eating

How Are Eating Disorders Treated?

Recovery is a long process. Treatment can take many months or even years of hard work. That is why many people with eating disorders have trouble sticking to their treatment. After a couple of weeks or so into the process, they may have a relapse and return to their unhealthy eating habits, such as bingeing and purging. In fact, it is not uncommon for people to begin treatment several times. It takes a lot of strength and determination, but most people with eating disorders

Who's Who?

Psychiatrists? Psychologists? Counselors? Dieticians? These are all health professionals who can help people with eating disorders. But what are the differences among them?

Psychiatrists are medical doctors. They are the only mental health professionals who can prescribe medications. They can provide talk therapy but usually rely on drugs and other medical treatments.

Psychologists are not licensed to prescribe medication. They usually have a degree in psychology from a university, rather than a degree from a medical school. Their special training allows them to test and diagnose patients and provide psychological counseling.

Social workers may provide psychological therapy or support for the patient's family. They can connect patients with support groups and get medical and other benefits for them.

Counselors have specialized training in particular areas of mental health. They provide psychological therapy and help patients work through their problems.

Nutritionists and dieticians are experts in food and nutrition. They examine the patient's eating habits and help to work out a plan for healthier living.

can recover. In general, about one third of people with anorexia recover completely after treatment, and another one third recover enough to get back to their daily activities but are still struggling. The last one third continue to suffer from anorexia and must be treated in the hospital from time to time.[6]

Refeeding: Take It Slow

The medical team has to act quickly when treating someone with severe anorexia nervosa. The patient needs plenty of food and water to help damaged body organs recover. That may mean feeding liquid nutrients through a tube into the stomach if the patient can't or won't eat regular food. But refeeding (restoring nutrients after starvation) can't go faster than the body can handle. Someone who has been taking in only 500 calories a day can't suddenly switch to the 3,000-calorie diet that may be needed for regaining weight. Usually the refeeding starts with many small meals a day, then is gradually increased. The goal is to get back to at least 90 percent of a healthy weight for that person. By then, many of the effects of starvation, such as inability to concentrate, irritability, and depression, go away. Once the medical emergency has been treated, psychological therapy can begin.

Eating disorders should be treated by health professionals who specialize in these conditions. Every person is different, so each treatment plan should be developed specifically for the individual. Since eating disorders may be caused by a number of factors, an effective treatment plan usually involves a combination of approaches. They should include the following:

Medical attention. Severe cases of anorexia nervosa may need immediate hospitalization in order to bring electrolyte levels back to a healthy balance, and feeding tubes may be necessary for weight gain.

Psychotherapy. Therapy is very important in the treatment process, since eating disorders are typically caused by hidden emotional problems and negative ways of thinking. Several types of psychotherapy (or "talk therapy") may be used to help people change their attitudes, emotions, and behavior patterns. They include:

- *Cognitive therapy,* aimed at identifying and changing the patient's mistaken ideas and beliefs, such as distorted body image and fear of food.

- *Behavior therapy,* focusing on changing harmful behaviors, such as starving or bingeing.

- *Psychodynamic therapy,* to help the patient to uncover and understand emotional problems that may be hidden causes of the eating disorder. It is based on the idea that patients use food as comfort to protect themselves from upsetting feelings, such as anger, frustration, and pain.

- *Family therapy,* which involves bringing the entire family together for the session, to work on specific problem areas. The goal is to help family members communicate better and give emotional support to the patient. It also helps in educating family members about eating disorders.

- *Group therapy,* which allows the patient to get support from people who are dealing with the same problems.

Nutritional counseling. A professional nutritionist or dietician can teach patients how to eat a healthy diet and manage their weight successfully. The counselor may also explain the various ways poor eating habits can damage the patient's body.

Eating disorders treatment centers. Treatment center programs are very effective because they are dedicated specifically to people with eating disorders. The health specialists work with each patient individually, and each patient has his or her own personal treatment plan. Treatments involve various types of therapy, nutritional counseling, and support groups. Some treatment centers may be residential: Patients live there and can be monitored day and night. Others may offer outpatient services, in which patients live at home and come in only for therapy or counseling sessions and group meetings.

Medication. Antidepressant drugs such as Prozac® may help some people with eating disorders. They may be used to relieve depression and anxiety that often occur in patients with eating disorders. Some of these drugs stimulate the appetite and may be used to help people with anorexia gain weight. Others decrease appetite and may be used to help people who binge.

Brazilian fashion model Ana Carolina Reston died of anorexia nervosa when she was just twenty-one years old. Her death sparked a controversy in the fashion industry about its use of extremely thin models.

7

Preventing Eating Disorders

I
N NOVEMBER 2006, the fashion industry was shaken up by the news that twenty-one-year-old Brazilian fashion model Ana Carolina Reston had died from complications of anorexia nervosa. At the time of her death, she weighed only 88 pounds (40 kg) for her 5-foot-7-inch (170 cm) frame. She was only thirteen years old when she started her modeling career. During her growing years, she lived in a world where being thin was required for success. Friends and family were worried about her weight, but she would get very upset when anybody would ask her to eat.[1] Ana's death brought further attention to the need for changes in the fashion industry's standard of using only extremely thin models.

No. 1 Supermodel

Thinness was not always in fashion. The 1950s fashion icon Marilyn Monroe would be considered overweight by today's fashion industry standards. The trend to be super thin actually started in the 1960s when British supermodel Twiggy Lawson became hugely popular. (The name "Twiggy" came from her long, skinny legs.) Soon, full-figured models were replaced with skinny ones.

Marilyn Monroe

"Twiggy" Lawson

Changing Public Opinion

People learn at a young age what society considers beautiful. Every day in the United States, they are bombarded with images of thin, attractive men and women on TV and in magazines. Teens and younger children want to look like them. If they don't look like these celebrities, they wonder if they are "normal." The truth is, these celebrities do not look like the average person.

So how can we change what people consider beautiful? One way to do that is to change how beauty is depicted in the media.

The fashion industry has been responding to criticisms by health experts and concerned parents. In September 2006, for example, a top fashion show in Spain set up a new guideline for models: No one with a BMI less than 18 could take part in the show. One model who was rejected had a BMI of only 16, which is equivalent to being 5 feet 10 inches (178 cm) tall and weighing less than 110 pounds (50 kg).

The fashion industry has been responding to criticisms by health experts and concerned parents. In September 2006, a top fashion show in Spain set up a new guideline for models: No one with a BMI less than 18 could take part in the show.

In 2007, after months of debate, officials of Brazil's big national show, São Paulo Fashion Week, set a minimum age of sixteen for models in the show. Before that, girls often began their modeling careers at thirteen. The organizers of Fashion Week said they had decided to set the age limit to protect the health of young models, whose bodies are still developing. A big factor in the decision was the death of supermodel Ana Carolina Reston, as well as the deaths of five other models that occurred in the weeks that followed. These deaths were all linked to anorexia nervosa. Similar minimum age limits were already in effect in other fashion centers, such as Paris and Milan.

The New York fashion world has not gone that far, however. The Council of Fashion Designers of America drew up a set of guidelines for the 2007 Fashion Week in New York City, aimed at promoting healthier behavior for models. They recommended teaching models about nutrition and eating disorders, banning models under age sixteen, providing healthy snacks backstage, and banning smoking and alcohol. They did not include BMI limits, though, saying that the BMI does not give a fair picture of models' health. The guidelines were just suggestions, not strict rules. A spokesperson for Anna Wintour, editor of the fashion magazine *Vogue*, said, "The feeling is that it is not realistic to dictate or impose rules on a huge fashion industry. However,

In the entertainment industry, changes are also occurring in the image of the "ideal woman." One of the biggest hits of the 2006–2007 television season in the United States was *Ugly Betty*.

The TV show *Ugly Betty*, starring America Ferrara, won an Emmy Award in 2007. The show is helping to change the American image of the "ideal woman" by featuring a main character with more confidence than fashion sense.

we do believe raising awareness and consciousness will go the furthest toward increasing people's sensitivities to the problem."[2]

In the entertainment industry, changes are also occurring in the image of the "ideal woman." One of the biggest hits of the 2006–2007 television season in the United States was *Ugly Betty*, a series starring America Ferrara. Her character worked at a fashion magazine but was far from the fashion "ideal." She was not skinny, wore thick glasses and braces, and was often criticized for her choice of clothes. Her strength and confidence won the hearts of audiences all over the country. In fact, America Ferrara won a 2007 Emmy Award for her performance in *Ugly Betty*. In her acceptance speech, Ferrara said, "It's such a beautiful message about beauty that lies deeper than what we see. . . . I hear from young girls on a daily basis how [the show] makes them feel worthy and lovable, that they have more to offer the world than they thought."[3] The *Ugly Betty* idea actually started in South America, with a series that ran from 1999 to 2001 in Colombia. Other versions of the show have appeared in various parts of the world, including Mexico, Spain, Germany, the Netherlands, Russia, and India.

Singer and actress Jennifer Hudson won an Academy Award for her role in the movie *Dreamgirls*. She felt her win was a victory for all full-figured women.

In early 2007, Jennifer Hudson won a Golden Globe and an Oscar for her role in the musical film *Dreamgirls.* It was a dream come true for Jennifer, who never gave up after being voted off *American Idol* in 2004. She felt like it was a win for full-figured women everywhere. She especially couldn't believe it when she was asked to appear on the cover of the March issue of *Vogue.* Her curvy, full-figured body brought a very different look to the ideals of beauty. "People usually think fat and ugly," says Kellie Brown, a spokeswoman for the plus-sized clothing chain Avenue. "Fat doesn't have to be ugly. Curviness doesn't have to be ugly. Who would look at Jennifer Hudson and say that she was unattractive?"[4] BJ Towe, executive editor of *Figure*, a fashion and lifestyle magazine for plus-sized women, believes that the trend could be changing: "I do think the American media is starting to realize this is who their audience is. That they're not all waif-thin."[5]

Awareness in Schools

Some schools in the United States have been trying to increase awareness of the dangers of eating disorders among young people. One video, entitled *Self-Image: The Fantasy, The Reality* from the popular PBS program for teenagers *In the Mix*, deals with America's obsession with body image. It discusses how the images teens see on television, in movies, in magazines, and on billboards drive them to diet excessively, develop dangerous eating habits, and have feelings of low self-esteem. The program allows for classroom discussions about the unrealistic body images in the media and the importance of developing self-confidence and self-worth. The video also gives advice on how to help or confront a friend with an eating disorder.

While some schools are actively working to prevent eating disorders, others are more concerned with the growing numbers of overweight and obese children. As of 2007, for example, schools in sixteen states were screening for overweight children and sending home report cards for those with high BMIs. Some health experts believe, however, that these reports give parents the wrong message. They may immediately put their children on an extreme diet and make them so afraid of eating "too much" that they develop eating disorders.

Some promising programs in elementary and middle schools are helping to develop healthy eating habits with a positive approach. Hundreds of schools are now using Planet Health, a program developed by Harvard

University researchers. Healthy messages about how exercise and nourishing foods can help the body are given in many different classes, not just "health ed." Math students, for example, may be asked to calculate how many hours in their lifetime they have spent sitting in front of a TV. Studies have shown that this program really works. Researchers found, for example, that after two years of Planet Health, middle-school girls were only half as likely to purge or use diet pills to control their weight as those in schools without the program.[6] The Coordinated Approach to Child Health (CATCH), used in 7,000 U.S. schools, also focuses on good health habits instead of weight. Gym activities keep all the students active, instead of standing around waiting for their turn. Color-coded "traffic light" codes ("go," "slow," and "whoa") on food choices in the cafeteria build on classes that teach kids to identify healthy and unhealthy foods.

Meanwhile, some health experts think that efforts to increase awareness of eating disorders among young people by stressing the danger may not be a good idea. They may actually encourage eating problems rather than helping to prevent them. Research has shown that teaching about eating disorders might introduce these

Spotlight: Girl Power

Dr. Catherine Steiner-Adair is concerned about how much time and energy girls spend worrying about their looks. She is a clinical psychologist who specializes in eating disorders among young girls and teens. For more than twenty-five years, she has been writing books and developing programs for schools on ways to build girls' self-esteem and help them to grow into confident, healthy adults.

Dr. Steiner-Adair has developed an interactive program, *Full of Ourselves: Advance in Girl Power, Health and Leadership*. It has been used as a curriculum in schools, after-school programs, summer camps, and weekly programs in libraries, churches, and synagogues. In upbeat, fun units, girls learn about healthy eating and exercise. They learn to spot ads and images on TV and in magazines that put too much importance on looks. The program also teaches healthy ways of dealing with emotions and stress. It builds leadership skills, as well. Each unit ends with a "call to action." Girls learn what to do if they see someone being put down or left out because of the way they look. They write letters to advertisers and editors of fashion magazines about the images they represent.

This program was tested on more than eight hundred girls in middle schools in five states. Tests showed that the curriculum brought about long-lasting positive changes in the girls' body image and self-esteem. It also increased their knowledge about health, nutrition, and discrimination against people who are considered overweight. It achieved better results than programs specifically aimed at preventing eating disorders.[7]

Dr. Steiner-Adair won the National Eating Disorders Association Prevention Award in 2005. She continues to work actively on a number of projects. In addition to her private practice as a clinical psychologist, she has worked with over 350 schools to develop educational and psychological programs. She is also a clinical instructor at Harvard Medical School, a director at the Klarman Eating Disorders Center, and a popular public speaker. She has appeared on *The Today Show*, *Good Morning America*, and the Discovery Channel, and has been featured in magazines including *Vogue*, *Seventeen*, and *Self*.[8]

behaviors to teenagers who had not considered them before. Rather, it would be better to teach them about accepting themselves and developing good self-esteem.

Eating Disorders Awareness and Prevention (EDAP) is an organization that has been dedicated to the prevention of eating disorders. One of the projects they help organize is National Eating Disorders Awareness Week (NEDAW), a yearly program that takes place on a number of college campuses across the country. Organizers call it a Body Fair. It includes a weeklong series of free events that are focused on helping to boost a person's self-esteem, while raising awareness about eating disorders at the same time. There are also fun activities that may include games to win prizes, massages, as well as free food, information booths, and free screening for possible eating disorders. In the end, the goal of NEDAW is to show how different everybody's size and shape is, and to respect and appreciate those differences. Another important message is that people need to ignore the media's images of the "ideal" and learn to feel good in their own skin.

Keeping a Healthy Weight

Health experts say that the best way to keep a healthy weight is through a balanced diet and physical activity.

People who are overweight can lose the extra pounds by cutting down the total amount of food they eat (especially foods high in

> Health experts say that the best way to keep a healthy weight is through a balanced diet and physical activity.

fats). They should eat enough to feel satisfied and aim to lose weight very gradually, a little at a time.

Food labels are very helpful in planning a balanced diet. They list the size of a serving and how many calories it contains. They also list the amounts of fat, protein, carbohydrates, and various vitamins and minerals in the food.

The U.S. Department of Agriculture has developed a food guide pyramid that places the foods we should eat every day into five main groups. The foods are grouped according to the nutrients they provide. The food groups are *(1) grains (bread, cereal, rice, and pasta)*; *(2) fruits; (3) vegetables; (4) milk, yogurt, and cheese*; and *(5) meat, poultry, fish, beans, eggs, and nuts.* A healthy diet should also include small amounts of fats and oils.

Exercise is just as important as a nutritious diet in staying healthy. Exercise can be any physical activity that you like to do, such as riding a bike, swimming,

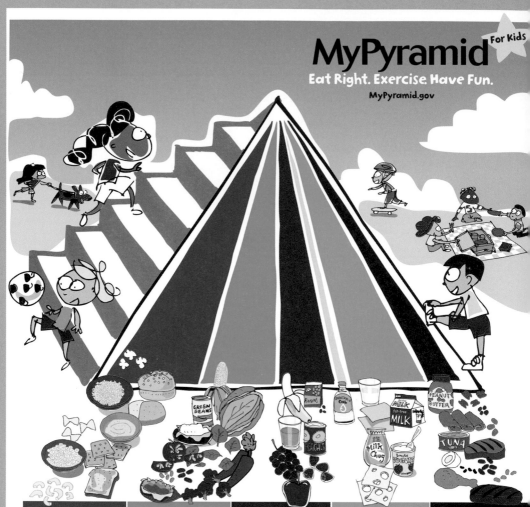

MyPyramid For Kids
Eat Right. Exercise. Have Fun.
MyPyramid.gov

Grains Make half your grains whole	**Vegetables** Vary your veggies	**Fruits** Focus on fruits	**Milk** Get your calcium-rich foods	**Meat & Beans** Go lean with protein
Start smart with breakfast. Look for whole-grain cereals. Just because bread is brown doesn't mean it's whole-grain. Search the ingredients list to make sure the first word is "whole" (like "whole wheat").	Color your plate with all kinds of great-tasting veggies. What's green and orange and tastes good? Veggies! Go dark green with broccoli and spinach, or try orange ones like carrots and sweet potatoes.	Fruits are nature's treats — sweet and delicious. Go easy on juice and make sure it's 100%.	Move to the milk group to get your calcium. Calcium builds strong bones. Look at the carton or container to make sure your milk, yogurt, or cheese is lowfat or fat-free.	Eat lean or lowfat meat, chicken, turkey, and fish. Ask for it baked, broiled, or grilled — not fried. It's nutty, but true. Nuts, seeds, peas, and beans are all great sources of protein, too.

For an 1,800-calorie diet, you need the amounts below from each food group. To find the amounts that are right for you, go to MyPyramid.gov.

Eat 6 oz. every day; at least half should be whole	Eat 2½ cups every day	Eat 1½ cups every day	Get 3 cups every day; for kids ages 2 to 8, it's 2 cups	Eat 5 oz. every day

Oils Oils are not a food group, but you need some for good health. Get your oils from fish, nuts, and liquid oils such as corn oil, soybean oil, and canola oil.

Find your balance between food and fun
- Move more. Aim for at least 60 minutes everyday, or most days.
- Walk, dance, bike, rollerblade — it all counts. How great is that!

Fats and sugars — know your limits
- Get your fat facts and sugar smarts from the Nutrition Facts label.
- Limit solid fats as well as foods that contain them.
- Choose food and beverages low in added sugars and other caloric sweeteners.

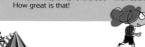
MyPyramid.gov
STEPS TO A HEALTHIER YOU

U.S. Department of Agriculture
Food and Nutrition Service
September 2005
FNS-381

USDA is an equal opportunity provider and employer

dancing, or playing soccer or tag. How much exercise is enough? Many studies show that thirty minutes most days is enough to make a difference; however, the U.S. Department of Agriculture recommends sixty minutes a day for children and teenagers. These "workouts" do not have to leave you sweating and huffing. Moderate exercise, such as walking, is fine. Even little changes in lifestyle, like taking the stairs instead of the elevator, or walking to a neighbor's house instead of getting a ride, can help.

Words to Live By

The National Eating Disorders Association gives some tips that can help kids eat healthfully and feel good about their choices.[9] They are words to live by.

Whether by yourself or with friends, find an activity you can get involved in. Any kind of exercise will make you healthier.

- Eat when you are hungry and stop when you feel full.

- There are no "good" or "bad" foods. All foods can be part of healthy eating. Eat a variety of foods, including whole grains, fruits, and vegetables. It is even okay to eat sweets and chips sometimes.

- If you are upset or angry or bored, look for something to do other than eating. It may also help to talk to a friend, parent, or teacher.

- Even if you aren't at the weight you'd like to be, you can be healthier and better able to do things if you exercise regularly and stay active. Try to find a sport or an activity that you like. Whether it's basketball or bowling, dancing or karate, join with a friend or practice by yourself and have fun.

- Having fun and feeling good about yourself go hand in hand. Try different hobbies other than sports, such as drawing, reading, playing music, or making things.

- Remember that healthy bodies and happy people come in many different shapes and sizes. No one body shape or body size is right for everybody.

- Don't tease people about being too fat, too thin, too short, or too tall. Teasing hurts and may lead to harmful behavior.

The bottom line is: Appreciate yourself. Don't worry about how you look. Just learn to like and respect yourself. Eat a variety of healthy foods, and enjoy being active.

Awareness of eating disorders has increased greatly since the 1970s. From the fashion industry to the entertainment world to schools throughout the world, this increased awareness has led to efforts to change the public's standards of beauty. Wider acceptance of individual differences should help to ease the pressure to be thin and cut down on unnecessary dieting. Meanwhile, research on eating disorders is revealing more about their causes, and more effective ways of treating them are being developed.

Questions and Answers

My friend keeps saying she hates her body. She is always trying one diet after another. Could she have an eating disorder? Possibly. Eating disorders often start with dieting. Keep an eye on her behavior. If she starts to skip meals, won't eat with friends, or looks very thin, try to urge her to get professional help. If she won't listen to you, talk to a responsible adult.

Sometimes I get so hungry! After I finish my dinner, I have to eat snacks. My mom is amazed at how much I eat. Could I have binge eating disorder? Probably not. Teenagers are known for having big appetites. You are growing and you need extra calories to fuel your growing body. If you find that you often eat a lot when you are feeling upset or angry, however, it could be a sign of an eating disorder.

What's the difference between bulimia and binge eating? Don't they both involve bingeing? Both conditions do involve bingeing (eating huge amounts of food). However, a bulimic will purge the food afterward. Binge eaters do not purge and are more likely to be overweight or obese.

How can you tell if somebody has bulimia? It is not easy because bulimics are very secretive. They are not usually very thin. Nor are they typically overweight, even though they often overeat. Some possible warning signs are: They spend a lot of time in the bathroom right after eating. You may find traces of vomit in the toilet or sink. They are constantly complaining about their body. You may find a bunch of candy wrappers in the wastebasket, or a secret stash of candy and snack foods in their bedroom. If you think someone close to you has bulimia, talk to a responsible adult about it.

My little sister is always comparing herself to her favorite female pop singers. She keeps telling me how fat she looks, but to me, she looks really skinny. She's only nine years old. She's too young to have an eating disorder, isn't she? Eating disorders are becoming increasingly common among young girls, even as young as six years old. Lots of kids complain about their looks, but that doesn't mean they have an eating disorder. If your sister starts dieting, it could be the start of a problem.

My brother is on the high school track team. He runs for four hours every day. He stays up late every night to work on his homework because he spends so much time exercising. He looks so worn out all the time. Could he have exercise bulimia? Athletes often feel the pressure to stay physically fit. When exercising starts to interfere with a person's life, it could be exercise bulimia. It sounds like your brother's compulsive exercising is affecting his health. He should get professional help.

Everybody keeps blaming the fashion industry and the media for causing eating disorders. If that's true, why do some people develop them and others don't? There is not one single cause for eating disorders. Usually a combination of factors are involved. Research has shown that heredity also plays a role. People who have inherited these genes may be more likely to develop an eating disorder after being teased about being chubby and feeling society's pressure to be thin.

Eating Disorders Timeline

383 .... Wealthy Roman women, trying to show the strength of their Christian faith, starve themselves; one dies, becoming the first recorded death from anorexia nervosa.

1380 .... Saint Catherine of Siena dies after starving and punishing herself to try to achieve purity.

1689 .... Richard Morton gives the first medical description of anorexia nervosa in his publication *Phthisiologia, or, a Treatise of Consumptions.*

1873 .... British physician Sir William Gull and French psychiatrist Ernest-Charles Lasègue independently describe anorexia nervosa; Dr. Gull gives anorexia nervosa its name.

1894 .... Psychiatrist Sigmund Freud describes a case of anorexia in a young woman.

1959 .... Psychiatrist Albert Stunkard identifies binge eating disorder.

1960s .... Supermodel Twiggy Lawson makes the super-skinny look popular, and becomes the first underweight woman to be considered as having the ideal body.

1979 .... British psychiatrist Gerald Russell is the first to describe bulimia.

1980 .... The American Psychiatric Association (APA) officially classifies eating disorders as mental illnesses in a standard reference guide, *The Diagnostic and Statistical Manual of Mental Disorders (DSM)*. Bulimia is classified as a separate condition in *DSM III*.

1983 .... Singer Karen Carpenter dies of complications due to anorexia, bringing public awareness to the disease for the first time.

1985 .... The Renfrew Center, opening in Philadelphia, becomes the country's first residential facility devoted specifically to the treatment of eating disorders.

1987 .... In *DSM III*, the term *bulimia* is replaced with *bulimia nervosa*.

1994 .... Binge eating disorder is officially recognized as a separate and distinct eating disorder.

2007 .... The McLean Hospital, an affiliate of Harvard Medical School, reports that binge eating disorder is more common than both anorexia and bulimia, as indicated in the first national survey on eating disorders.

For More Information

The American Anorexia/Bulimia Association of Philadelphia
E-mail: jbsmje@epix.net
Phone: (215) 221-1864
Web site: http://www.aabaphila.org/

American Dietetic Association
120 South Riverside Plaza, Suite 2000
Chicago, IL 60606-6995
Phone: (800) 877-1600
Web site: http://www.eatright.org

Mental Health America
2000 N. Beauregard Street, 6th Floor
Alexandria, VA 22311
Toll-free: (800) 969-6642
Web site: http://www.nmha.org

National Alliance for Mental Illness (NAMI)
Colonial Place Three
2107 Wilson Blvd., Suite 300
Arlington, VA 22201-3042
Phone: (703) 524-7600
Info. Helpline: (800) 950-NAMI (6264)
Web site: http://www.nami.org

National Association of Anorexia Nervosa and Associated
Disorders (ANAD)
P.O. Box 7
Highland Park, IL 60035
E-mail: anad20@aol.com
Phone: (847) 831-3438
Web site: http://www.anad.org/site/anadweb/

National Eating Disorders Association (NEDA)
603 Stewart St., Suite 803
Seattle, WA 98101
E-mail: info@NationalEatingDisorders.org
Phone: (206) 382-3587
Toll-free: (800) 931-2237
Web site: http://www.edap.org/

National Hopeline Network
24-hour crisis hotline
Toll-free: (800) SUICIDE (784-2433)

Overeaters Anonymous
World Service Office
P.O. Box 44020
Rio Rancho, NM 87174-4020
E-mail: info@oa.org
Phone: (505) 891-2664
Web site: http://www.oa.org/

The Renfrew Center Foundation for Eating Disorders

475 Spring Lane
Philadelphia, PA 19128
E-mail: foundation@renfrew.org
Toll-free: (877) 367-3383
Fax: (215) 482-2695
Web site: http://www.renfrew.org

Suicide Prevention Action Network USA (SPAN USA)

1025 Vermont Avenue, NW, Suite 1066
Washington, DC 20005
E-mail: info@spanusa.org
Hotline: (800) 273-TALK (8255)
Phone: (202) 449-3600
Web site: http://www.spanusa.org

Chapter Notes

Chapter 1. A Battle With Food

1. Peg Tyre, "No One to Blame," *Newsweek*, December 5, 2005, pp. 50–59.

2. "Eating Disorders 101 Guide: A Summary of Issues, Statistics and Resources," The Renfrew Center Foundation for Eating Disorders, revised October 2003, <http://www.renfrewcenter.com/uploads/resources/ 1067338472_1.doc> (January 23, 2007).

3. "Let's Talk Facts About Eating Disorders," American Psychiatric Association, 2005, <http://www. healthyminds.org/multimedia/eatingdisorders.pdf> (June 5, 2007).

4. "Eating Disorders 101 Guide: A Summary of Issues, Statistics and Resources."

5. Tyre, p. 52.

Chapter 2. Understanding Eating Disorders

1. Jamie-Lynn Sigler and Sheryl Berk, *Wise Girl: What I've Learned About Life, Love, and Loss* (New York: Pocket Books, 2002), p. 24; Jamie-Lynn Sigler, "Exercising Control," *People*, May 27, 2002, p. 70.

2. Sigler, p. 70.

3. Sigler and Berk.

4. " 'Sopranos' Daughter Jamie-Lynn Discala to Deliver Open VISIONS Forum Lecture," *Fairfield University*, August 20, 2004, <http://www.fairfield.edu/ x3586.html> (May 18, 2007).

5. Mark Schwed, "Justine Time," *TV Guide*, November 9, 1996, pp. 28–29.

6. "Eating Disorders 101 Guide: A Summary of Issues, Statistics and Resources," The Renfrew Center Foundation for Eating Disorders, revised October 2003, <http://www.renfrewcenter.com/uploads/resources/1067338472_1.doc> (January 23, 2007).

7. Tracey D. Wade, Cynthia M. Bulik, Michael Neale, and Kenneth S. Kendler, "Anorexia and Major Depression: Shared Genetic and Environmental Risk Factors," *American Journal of Psychiatry*, March 2000, <http://www.ajp.psychiatryonline.org/cgi/reprint/157/3/469> (February 12, 2007).

Chapter 3. What Is Anorexia?

1. Peg Tyre, "No One to Blame," *Newsweek*, December 5, 2005, pp. 55, 58.

2. U.S. Department of Health and Human Services and U.S. Department of Agriculture, "Dietary Guidelines for Americans, 2005," p. 23 (pamphlet), <http://www.health.gov/dietaryguidelines/dga2005/document/pdf/dga2005.pdf> (June 13, 2007).

3. U.S. Department of Health and Human Services, "Nutrition—Healthy Eating," Girlshealth.gov, updated April 2006, <http://www.girlshealth.gov/nutrition/weight.htm> (February 16, 2007).

4. "Eating & Weight Disorders Program at Mount Sinai," *The Mount Sinai Medical Center*, © 2000–2007, <http://www.mountsinai.org/msh/msh_frame.jsp?url=clinical_services/eatingdisorders.htm> (June 7, 2007).

Chapter 4. What Is Bulimia?

1. Sandy Fertman Ryan, "The Perfect Girl," *Girl's Life*, August/September 2004, pp. 66–67, <http://www.thinforlife.info/cgi-bin/mojonews/news.cgi?act=read&cat=2&num=5> (February 7, 2007).

2. Ibid.

3. Ibid.

4. "Eating Disorders 101 Guide: A Summary of Issues, Statistics and Resources," The Renfrew Center Foundation for Eating Disorders, revised October 2003, <http://www.renfrewcenter.com/uploads/resources/1067338472_1.doc> (January 23, 2007).

5. "Statistics: How Many People Have Eating Disorders?" Anorexia Nervosa and Related Eating Disorders, Inc. (ANRED), updated February 6, 2007, <http://www.anred.com/stats.html> (February 19, 2007).

Chapter 5. What Is Binge Eating Disorder?

1. Jill Smolowe, "Everything to Lose," *People Magazine*, November 4, 2002, p. 60.

2. Ibid.

3. Ibid., p. 63.

4. Ibid., pp. 58–63.

5. McLean Hospital, "First National Survey on Eating Disorders Finds Binge Eating More Common Than Other Eating Disorders," Press Release, February 1, 2007, <http://www.mclean.harvard.edu/news/press/current.php?id=103> (February 23, 2007).

6. Centers for Disease Control and Prevention, "BMI—Body Mass Index: About BMI for Adults," reviewed February 8, 2007, <http://www.cdc.gov/nccdphp/dnpa/bmi/adult_BMI/about_adult_BMI.htm> (March 1, 2007).

7. Centers for Disease Control and Prevention, "Prevalence of Overweight and Obesity Among Adults: United States 2003-2004," reviewed January 30, 2007, <http://www.cdc.gov/nchs/products/pubs/pubd/hestat s/overweight/overwght_adult_03.htm> (March 2, 2007).

8. Ibid.

9. Centers for Disease Control and Prevention, "Obesity Still a Major Problem," *National Center for Health Statistics*, April 14, 2006, <http://www.cdc.gov/nchs/pressroom/06facts/obesity03_04.htm> (March 2, 2007).

10. Centers for Disease Control and Prevention, "Prevalence of Overweight Among Children and Adolescents: United States 1999-2002," reviewed January 11, 2007, <http://www.cdc.gov/nchs/products/pubs/pubd/hestats/overwght99.htm> (March 2, 2007).

Chapter 6. Diagnosis and Treatment

1. Ericka Sóuter, "My Secret Struggle," *People*, July 3, 2006, p. 54.

2. Ibid., p. 56.

3. Ibid., p. 54.

4. Ibid., pp. 54–57.

5. Steven Reinberg, "Hair Analysis May Help Detect Eating Disorders," *HealthCentral*, October 16, 2006, <http://www.healthcentral.com/newsdetail/408/535513.html> (March 7, 2007).

6. Laurel Mayer, "Body Composition and Anorexia Nervosa: Does Physiology Explain Psychology?" *The American Journal of Clinical Nutrition*, Vol. 73, 2001, pp. 851–852, <http://www.ajcn.org/cgi/content/full/73/5/851> (June 13, 2007).

Chapter 7. Preventing Eating Disorders

1. "Anorexia Takes a Life," *People*, December 4, 2006, p. 120; Gabe Guarente, "A Model's Anorexic Death," *Us Weekly*, December 4, 2006, p. 16.

2. Eric Wilson, "Health Guidelines Suggested for Models," *The New York Times*, January 6, 2007, p. C1, <http://www.nytimes.com/2007/01/06/business/06thin.html?ex=1181880000&en=829214b5e6f0a60c&ei=5070> (June 13, 2007).

3. Golden Globe Award Show, January 15, 2007.

4. Tanika White, "Curves Could Be Coming Back Into Vogue," *The Star-Ledger* (Newark, New Jersey), March 9, 2007, p. 57.

5. Ibid., p. 63.

6. S.B. Austin, et al., "The Impact of a School-Based Obesity Prevention Trial on Disordered Weight-Control Behaviors in Early Adolescent Girls," *Archives of Pediatrics and Adolescent Medicine*, March 2005, pp. 225–230.

7. Catherine Steiner-Adair and Lisa Sjostrom, "Full of Ourselves: Advancing Girl Power, Health & Leadership, Jewish Women and the Feminist Revolution (Jewish Women's Archive), © 2005, <www.jwa.org/feminism/_html/_pdf/JWA068a.pdf> (March 15, 2007).

8. "Catherine Steiner-Adair," Harry Walker Agency, © 2005, <http://www.harrywalker.com/speakers_template.cfm?Spea_ID=1005&SubcatID=198> (March 15, 2007).

9. "Tips for Kids on Eating Well and Feeling Good about Yourself," National Eating Disorders Association, © 2006, <http://www.nationaleatingdisorders.org/p.asp?WebPage_ID=286&Profile_ID=69224> (March 10, 2007).

Glossary

amenorrhea—A lack of menstrual periods after puberty.

anorexia nervosa—An eating disorder in which a person is obsessed with being thin and refuses to eat enough food to stay healthy.

binge—Eat unusually large amounts of food; a period of eating large amounts of food.

binge eating disorder—An eating disorder in which a person eats unusually large amounts of food with no control over his or her behavior. Food is not purged; often linked with obesity; also called **compulsive overeating**.

body image—The way a person sees his or her body or body size.

body mass index (BMI)—A ratio of weight to height that indicates how much body fat a person has.

bulimia nervosa—An eating disorder in which a person overeats then vomits, takes laxatives, or exercises to get rid of the excess calories; commonly called **bulimia** for short.

calorie—A unit of measurement for the amount of energy stored in foods.

cholecystokinin (CCK)—A hormone that is released by cells in the intestines after a meal, and signals to the satiety center in the hypothalamus controlling the level of appetite (indicating a person is "full").

cholesterol—A fatty substance important for brain growth; excessive amounts may clog arteries.

compulsive overeating—See *binge eating disorder.*

diabetes—A condition in which the body cannot store and use sugar properly, resulting in dangerously high amounts of sugar in the blood.

dieting—Eating reduced amounts of food, or avoiding certain kinds of food, to lose weight.

dietician—A health professional who specializes in nutrition.

fasting—Not eating any food at all.

food pyramid—A diagram showing healthy exercise levels and the kinds of foods and the amounts of each kind that should be eaten in a balanced diet.

genes—Chemicals inside cells that determine which traits will be passed on from one generation to the next.

hormones—Chemicals that help to control and regulate the body's activities.

hypothalamus—A part of the brain containing control centers for body functions, including body temperature, sleep/wake cycles, emotions, and appetite.

menstrual period—A flow of blood that occurs in an adult female about once a month as part of her reproductive cycle.

neurotransmitter—A chemical that carries messages from one part of the brain to another.

nutrients—Chemicals in foods used by the body.

obesity—A condition in which large amounts of stored fat put a strain on the body; being seriously overweight.

obsessive-compulsive disorder (OCD)—A psychological disorder in which a person performs tasks repeatedly without any control over his or her behavior, or thinks continually about upsetting topics.

ostcoporosis—A condition in which the bones have less calcium than normal, become weak, and break easily.

psychotherapy—"Talk therapy"; treatment involving a variety of techniques that help people to change their attitudes, emotions, and behavior patterns.

puberty—A period of rapid growth and changes in the body in preparation for adulthood.

purge—To get rid of food from the body through excessive methods including vomiting; taking laxatives, ipecac syrup, or diuretics; and overexercising.

refeeding—Restoring nutrients after starvation.

self-esteem—The ability to value oneself; to feel confident; and to feel satisfied with oneself.

self-image—A person's opinion of his or her own appearance, abilities, and personality.

serotonin—A neurotransmitter that controls hunger, sleep, impulse control, anger, depression, anxiety, and perception.

Further Reading

Echevarría, Darah. *So Now You Know: The Battle of a Teenage Girl Fighting Her Eating Disorders in Silence*. London: Athena Press, 2004.

Lawton, Sandra Augustyn (ed.). *Eating Disorders Information for Teens*. Detroit, Mich.: Omnigraphics, 2005.

Kolodny, Nancy J. *The Beginner's Guide to Eating Disorders Recovery*. Carlsbad, Calif.: Gürze Books, 2004.

Sigler, Jamie-Lynn, and Sheryl Berk. *Wise Girl: What I've Learned About Life, Love, and Loss*. New York: Pocket Books, 2002.

Trueit, Trudi Strain. *Eating Disorders*. New York: Scholastic, 2003.

Internet Addresses

Centers for Disease Control and Prevention. *BMI—Body Mass Index.* "Child and Teen Calculator."
http://apps.nccd.cdc.gov/dnpabmi/Calculator.aspx

National Institutes of Health. *MedlinePlus.* "Eating Disorders."
http://www.nlm.nih.gov/medlineplus/eatingdisorders.html

WebMD. *Understanding Eating Disorders in Teens.*
http://www.webmd.com/a-to-z-guides/understanding-eating-disorders-teens

U.S. Department of Agriculture (USDA), "My Food Guide Pyramid"
http://www.mypyramid.gov/
Figure out the amounts of food and exercise you need every day.

Index

A

adolescence, 28–29, 45

amenorrhea, 45

anorexia nervosa
    brain effects, 43, 45–46
    development, family
      issues in, 34
    development of, 17–21
    diagnosis, 76–80
    eating rituals, 39
    exercise issues, 19–20, 41
    genetic risk of, 32
    health effects, 41–46
    prevention, 7
    profile, 6–7, 15
    public awareness of, 23
    recovery rates, 82
    statistics, 63
    symptoms/signs, 7, 9–10,
      35–41
    treatment, 7, 10–11, 21,
      82, 83

antidepressants, 49, 85

anxiety
    brain control in, 45, 46
    bulimia and, 54
    treatment, 85

appetite, 37, 62

athletes, 41, 107

B

Bateman, Justine, 24–26

behavior therapy, 83

binge eating disorder
    diagnosis, 76–80, 105
    health effects, 69–60
    prevention, 7
    profile, 6–7, 15–16
    statistics, 63
    symptoms/signs, 7, 60–64
    treatment, 7, 49–50, 61

bingeing, 6, 15, 51–56

blood pressure issues, 69

BMI (Body Mass Index),
    66–67, 90

Body Fair, 98

body image
    in eating disorder
      development, 13–15,
      26–29, 47, 95
    positive, enhancing, 97
    public opinion and,
      88–94
    super-skinny look
      popularity, 16, 87–88

Body Mass Index (BMI),
    66–67, 90

brain
    control, of eating, 37
    effects, of
      anorexia/bulimia on,
      43, 45–46, 57, 59

bulimia nervosa
    brain effects, 45–46, 57,
      59
    diagnosis, 71–80,
      105–107
    exercise, 52, 53, 58, 107

menstrual periods, 45, 58–59
Monroe, Marilyn, 88

N

National Eating Disorders
    Association, 22, 32
National Eating Disorders
    Awareness Week (NEDAW),
    98
neurotransmitters, 45–46, 59
NHANES study, 65–69
nutritionists, 81, 84

O

obesity
    in binge eating disorder,
        60–64
    defined, 64–69
    health effects, 69–60
    school screening, 95
    statistics, 65–69
obsessive-compulsive disorder
    (OCD), 39
osteoarthritis, 70
osteoporosis, 44–45, 59
overweight defined, 64–69

P

Planet Health, 95–96
proteins, 38
Prozac (fluoxetine), 85
psychiatrists, 81
psychodynamic therapy, 83–84
psychologists, 81
psychotherapy, 83–84
puberty, 28–29, 45
purging, 6, 15, 48–49, 51–56

R

refeeding, 82
Renfrew Center Foundation
    for Eating Disorders, 27
Reston, Ana Carolina, 87, 90

S

satiety center, 37
self-esteem, 27–29, 50, 95–98,
    103
*Self-Image: The Fantasy, The
    Reality,* 94–95
serotonin, 45–46, 59
Sigler, Jamie-Lynn, 17–23
skin effects, 44, 58
social workers, 81
starvation
    effects of, 41–46, 82
    as religious ritual, 42
Steiner-Adair, Catherine, 97
substance abuse, 54
suicidal thoughts, 20, 49–50,
    54

T

talk therapy, 83–84
teasing, 33, 60, 103
television, 101
treatment centers, 84–85
type 2 diabetes, 69

U

Ugly Betty, 90–92

W

wasting away, 43
weight, maintaining, 98–104